—A—
LIFE'S
WORK

*Learning to Overrule
My Mindless Brain*

—— SHEP MCKENNEY ——

A LIFE'S WORK

Cover and Interior Design by
Transcendent Publishing
PO Box 66202
St. Pete Beach, FL 33707
www.transcendentpublishing.com

TRANSCENDENT
publishing

Paperback ISBN: 979-8-9857704-8-3
Hardcover ISBN: 979-8-9857704-9-0

Printed in the United States of America.

DEDICATION

To Pat, who turned on the lights

TABLE OF CONTENTS

INTRODUCTION

For most of my life, I've searched in vain to find a way to be at peace with myself and the world around me – in other words, to be happy.

It hasn't been for want of trying, or, for that matter, the outward markers of a good life. I have had, not just professional success and the wealth and possessions that go with it, but a loving wife, children, and grandchildren, in addition to a satisfying circle of friends. My health has been excellent. On the outside, I've been good.

On the inside, however, I haven't been good, but flooded with a torrent of distracting, unwanted fears and speculations and burdened by an inner inertia that kept me from doing the things I knew were good for me. It wasn't that I didn't know how I wanted to be, or what I wanted to do, but that there was something inside me that was actively working against me.

I've led two parallel lives – calm, collected and complete on the outside, and desperately trying to figure out what the hell was wrong on the inside. In the event, I had to come to grips with where "hell" was. And, when I did that, it became obvious what Heaven was.

What I came to realize is that hell is in my anxious, foot-dragging, drama-queen brain and that Heaven is what is left when I can keep that machine from doing what I don't want it to do and get it to do what I do want it to do. And that Heaven isn't just a relief, but opens the way to the fantastic peace and beauty that religion, at its best, has always promised. Yet, unlike classical religious heavens, the one I will describe is not a permanent future residence, but a present hotel that I check in and out of depending on how well I can manage my brain.

I've also come to realize that my getting into Heaven does not require sitting on a cushion on a mountaintop, ascending to some superior realm, abandoning the messy, striving exterior world. I want to be an active participant in that world, which is interesting and fulfilling. I just want my achievements to be informed by the best part of me, and not the other way around.

These realizations have inspired me to write this book about how our computer brains limit our ability to be happy. It is not an easy subject to write about.

One difficulty is that we know from medical science that our brains are the indispensable actuator of our every thought and movement. How can happiness be somewhere else? My considered answer to that question is that science cannot explain everything, and certainly not the most important things, and it cannot be allowed to become another monotheism – an exclusive explanation for everything that is - and thus limit our view of what a human life can be, just as historical monotheisms have done.

There is, however, a crucial scientific element here. I will advance the notion that, for the first time in human history, we have the scientific knowledge to understand how our brains, for all their indispensability, are agnostic tools that don't care about their owners except at the most physical, existential level. I do this by calling on the science of evolution, neuroscience, and computer science to explain why and how our brains were purposely built to achieve a mission that is no longer our own. That mission – like the mission of lower animals today – was to put its owner on track to arrive at a narrowly-defined destination – surviving long enough to reproduce in order to pass their genes on to the next generation. But our mission in the modern industrialized world is not to be on a track to a *certain* destination, but to discover happiness, which is a rolling, always changing, *uncertain* experience. So when we ask our brains to get off track, they're derailed. And that's why, I believe, our lives so often feel like a train wreck.

But the greatest difficulty in delivering this message is that I am trying to introduce the reader to a fundamentally different way to think about how to experience value in their life. That is sacred, closely guarded space, not easily penetrated. So, for example, when I call upon the teachings of religion, for the nonbeliever it can be a distracting reference to an archaic mythology that confuses more than it clarifies, and for the believer, the exclusive key to the kingdom, leaving my ideas irrelevant. I am trying to navigate a minefield of precious predilections and prejudices.

My way of getting past this difficulty is to speak in terms so intimately personal that conceptual ideas are bypassed. I do this by offering up the deepest, darkest parts of my interior autobiography, inviting the reader to do the same. My hope is that by the time you have finished this book you will know me in a way that you may not even know yourself. Mostly unwittingly, we shield ourselves and others from the madness within us and I want to rip away that shield. One of the main themes here is that life is lived on the inside, not on the outside, so that if you can bring yourself to go through the deeply humbling experience of acknowledging how crazy it is in there, you can get underneath your preconceptions and down to bedrock.

And what is that bedrock? It is what makes life worth living *at all*. It is at the heart of every decent religious tradition and self-help book and it is this: Each of us, independent of our genetic makeup or personal life situation, has the innate power to create happiness for ourselves and others. It is so obvious that it is reduced to platitudes. I will pick three:

"Live in the present"; "See the glass as half full, not half empty"; and "Do unto others as you would have them do unto you."

Yet, it is one thing to endorse these platitudes and entirely another to incorporate them into your life from moment to moment because there is so much distracting noise in our brains – speculating, fearing, grasping – *mindless*. And because that noise is so loud, it drowns out the still small voice within us that asks this question: "Who do you want to be right now?" The "right now" part is important because that still small voice sits there patiently waiting to be asked, while the brain is quick to urge and insist, preempting the question and hijacking our consciousness.

Constant awareness of that opportunity is crucial because you can't make a choice if you don't realize you have one. The default when you're unhappy is "that's just the way I am", and the opportunity is, "No, that's not the way I am, that's the way my brain is, and if it doesn't care about me I've got to care about myself."

What follows is an account of how I have come to this way of thinking, how I have used it to make my life better and the potential I believe it has for others.

CHAPTER ONE

Jesus is coming – look busy.

George Carlin

The Sunday school teacher was exhorting my fellow eight-year-olds and me to be virtuous and not to do harm to others. He said that even evil done in private would not go unpunished, because God was always looking down on us – kind of like a blimp hovering over a football stadium – and He didn't miss anything. The teacher then told the story of a boy who saw a songbird sitting in a tree and, after checking to see that no one was watching, picked up a rock and threw it at the bird, killing it. The teacher intoned that even in killing a tiny songbird, the boy had sinned in the eyes of God and would be called to account.

My only (silent) reaction was, *Wow, I wish I could throw a rock like that!*

What I saw in church seemed remote, as if I was looking at it through a thick pane of glass. I was told to worship a perfect Jesus, who was depicted as a man wrapped in a sheet, with long hair and a scraggly beard, living in a semi-desert, a long time ago. The value of my life was remote too – how I would be judged on that distant Judgment Day.

At school the emphasis was on worshiping an idealized future result as well. Becoming a doctor or a lawyer was regarded as being particularly lofty – those people lived in big houses and drove nice cars. They actually talked about "molding" children for the part they would play in the future. The repeated homily was, "Set your goals high so that if you fall short you'll still have attained something."

My dad's persona fit right in with the message at school, instilling the fear of falling short in my brothers and me. He was the breadwinner, the person we depended upon to survive, and the rest of us, including my mother, deferred to his wishes and what he had to say. And what he had to say was that it was cold and competitive out there in the man's world, and my brothers and I had better prepare ourselves to face it – a message reinforced when, in periodic explosions of rage, he would throw my older brothers on the floor and brutally whip them with his belt for their failure to stay out of trouble and get decent grades.

I stayed out of trouble and got good grades.

But I knew that I didn't want to live under the yoke of fear, that my life had value in the present and that miracles didn't just happen in the Middle East two thousand years ago.

I am seven years old and staying at my grandparents' farm for the day. My grandfather takes me to the creek that runs through the farm to a wooden rowboat tethered to an oak tree. The May sun is warm and the air has that pregnant quality that is the peculiar province of spring mornings. I sit in the front of the boat and he stands in the back and takes us down the creek, the ash push pole moving rhythmically up and down in his hands as we glide over the gin-clear water and past the marsh grass with its purple and white hibiscus blossoms and warbling red-winged blackbirds.

My grandfather says nothing, and as I look ahead it seems as if I am alone on a magic carpet, yet taken care of and safe. As we approach the fish trap we have come to tend, the boat swings around and we both reach into the water and pull the net up until the mesh chamber where the fish are concentrated comes over the side in an explosion of wet iridescence. Sunfish, bass, pickerel and perch spill into the bottom of the boat, radiating every color of the rainbow in the brilliant light.

The sight at my feet stuns me, and suddenly my body seems to change form, and I am looking down, not from four feet, but a hundred feet, a thousand feet. My size is infinite, and everything – the boat, the creek, my grandfather – has fallen away, leaving only the fish and me.

I didn't tell anyone about my experience with my grandfather, afraid that no one would take it seriously. I could hardly believe it myself.

As I approached puberty, I had another epiphany that I told no one about.

In my sixth-grade class, most of the children lived in rural areas like my own, which comprised most of the school district. My classmate Chuck, however, lived on the edge of a wealthy suburb and had a number of city friends who went to a different school. When Chuck invited me to a party at his house I was not sure what to expect, because I had never been to a kid's party that was not a birthday party. When I arrived, I was greeted by his mother, who was young and pretty with a smile that suggested a permissiveness I was not used to in parents.

The children at the party were well-dressed and seemed a lot more confident than I felt. I tried to fit in as best I could, and before long was involved in a game I knew only by reputation – spin the bottle. About a dozen kids, evenly mixed between boys and girls, sat in a circle, with a bottle set on its side in the middle. The bottle would be spun, and whomever the neck pointed to would select a boy and then a girl to go into an adjoining room and kiss.

The time came when the bottle pointed to me and then to a cute, almost doll-like dark-haired girl. She looked into my eyes, took me by the hand, led me into the room, and closed the door behind us. When she turned to face me, she put her hands on the sides of my face, slowly tilted her head and, with slightly parted lips, kissed me on the mouth for a long, long second.

As she turned away to rejoin the game, already focused on her next conquest, I stood dazed, vibrating like a tuning fork, unmoving, unable to move, not knowing what had happened, but thrilled in a way that left me changed forever.

I lived in two worlds. The first one resembled the primitive world in which my brain was designed. In that world children were a burden in the present, their value measured by how well they could be molded into effective tribal team members as adults.

The second world – the one I wanted to live in – was built on present interior experience rather than future external results. It wasn't that I didn't understand that effort and discipline were required on my part to provide a foundation for my future existence, but what was missing was that no one was talking about what, to me, were the best parts of life. That part couldn't be molded, or even intended, but was simply opening up to all that is good and beautiful in life.

The first world was after the pot of gold at the end of the rainbow. The second was just enthralled with the rainbow.

CHAPTER TWO

Why are all you whiteys such tight-asses?

Richard Pryor

I had to find a place in the world as I found it. That was not easy, because I had little confidence in my ability to compete. Small in stature, with no particular physical gifts, I felt inadequate athletically and romantically. When they chose up sides for softball, I was one of the last ones picked. As for the girls, I think my anxiety must have been a turnoff. My feelings of inadequacy were not just built on my existing self-image, but on my seeming inability to take positive steps to improve my life. Yet, I knew at the time what those positive steps were and that if I took them my life would be better. Working out, athletic training, learning to dance, telling the girls you like them and want them is pretty straightforward stuff. But I was so consumed by a destructive fear that I would fail that I couldn't bring myself to try. My brain wouldn't let me do the logical thing.

Since I didn't think I could win, my strategy became not losing. I pretended that I didn't care about athletics or girls, thus cutting myself off from most of adolescent society. I joined the debate team, not because I liked arguing, but because it was the only place I felt I could compete. I morphed into a nerdy kind of know-it-all, putting up a façade to hide my fear and despair. Not able to win on their terms, I would see my classmates as inferiors whose standards didn't apply to me, and I let them know it, desperately wanting them to see the value in me even as I gave them no chance to do so. I knew I didn't want to be that unattractive person, didn't want to feel inferior and afraid, *but I couldn't seem to help myself.* Defending that façade became a program in my brain that, in ways large and small, polluted my relationship with my fellow human beings throughout my formative years.

I did have one high school friend, Larry, who somehow saw through all that, even as he was everything I was not. The son of a rigidly formal bank president, Larry did everything right and checked off all the boxes. He was conscientiously successful as a student and athlete, popular across the spectrum of the student body, and became its president. Looking back after all these years, his perfection seems unreal. He was handsome, the neatest-dressing male I ever knew, and his handwriting looked almost like printing. However, this perfection was not a turn-off to others, including the girls, and I remember the prettiest girl in the class throwing herself at his feet.

Yet Larry liked me, wanted to do things with me, and made no secret of the fact that I was one of his best friends, which must have been a mystery to everyone else. How could he see through all my fear and defensiveness? I can only say that he saw something in me that no one else seemed to see, and gave me hope that I could find a place in the world.

But there was another world around me – literally on my doorstep – that I could never be a part of. They were the Negroes.

My childhood home in Southeastern Virginia was next to a mill town called Bell's Mill, and although most of the people who lived around us were black, they were, for the most part, totally separate from us, culturally if not physically. There was no hostility in it; they just didn't count, were simply part of the environment, like the heat in the summer or the flatness of the countryside.

It was not as if I didn't have any contact with black people. At my dad's gas station, I pumped gas after school and worked beside John Henry and Bryant, two middle-aged black men who handled tire repair and oil changes. While they didn't discuss the details of their private lives with a wet-behind-the-ears white boy, I overheard enough of their exchanges with the black customers to know they took themselves a lot less seriously than white people.

They even seemed to enjoy their religion. If you went by their churches on Sunday night and heard them singing, you knew there was nothing halfhearted in it. Even though they didn't have the things we had, they seemed to be enjoying their lives more. But there was nothing I could learn from them. Wasn't the object of life to get richer?

The only time the black culture could break through to me was when I had no time to raise my defenses.

Many summer days of my childhood were spent fishing from a bridge over a creek that crossed the road on which we lived. When I walked this road to the bridge, often there were black people walking the same road, but we followed the local practice of not speaking to or even looking at each other once we got close.

One Sunday afternoon when I was thirteen, I was headed toward the bridge when I saw coming towards me on the other side of the road a group of about a dozen or so black boys and girls my own age, all dressed up and obviously headed for an afternoon church service. They were in high spirits, talking and laughing loudly and, sensing that this encounter could be different, I stared woodenly ahead like some tobacco store Indian.

When they came abreast of me, one of the boys called out, "Hey, white boy." My worst fears realized, I had no choice but to look at them.

Smiling broadly, he called out, "You want some pussy?" Now they all laughed uproariously, particularly the girls. As their laughing died away, I picked up my pace, looking ahead again, stunned and mortified.

But, more than that, I was *envious*. Could it be that good? Could something so wonderful and exciting actually be brought out into the open to be not just acknowledged, but joked about?

These people, whose life situation was the very opposite of what I was told to aspire to, seemed to have such an easy relationship with something that exerted an almost gravitational pull on me. In fact, it would be hard to overstate how consumed I was by sex as a teenager, constantly fantasizing and masturbating. The only thing harder to overstate is how confused I was by it, overtaken by forces I could not understand or acknowledge. If the adult world was foisting a mechanical blueprint on me, at least I could see them acting it out. But sex was a secret, surfacing only as sin and shame, as when a teenager got pregnant. How was it that the most exciting thing to be shared with another person couldn't be talked about?

In the event, church was what allowed me to answer the challenge of that black teenager on Bell's Mill Road. The reason was Janice, my girlfriend for the last year of high school, whose family was a member of a stridently fundamentalist Christian sect. One of the good things about Janice was that her religion regarded dancing as the devils play. Since I didn't know how to dance and was afraid to make a fool of myself by trying, Janice provided cover when social occasions involved dancing.

There was another advantage. While Janice's parents were stricter than most about dating rules, they did encourage her and her friends to attend the frequent weeknight services at their church. That meant that I got to drive her to the services, detouring on the way home to park on the canal bank, where I learned, to my joy, that she was quite experienced in matters of sex. Bookish and shy outwardly, she was patient and kind, almost motherly, in our intimate relations, seemingly never turned off by my pent-up over eagerness. And when, in my lustful enthusiasm, I would say that I would love her forever, she let me know that was not to be, reminding me, in so many words, to just be present.

These totally unexpected experiences with Larry, those black kids and Janice were my *life*, and yet I couldn't acknowledge them to an outside world that was constantly reminding me what I should do and become. While I couldn't have articulated it at the time, there was a part of me that just wanted to yell at all those authority figures out there, *"Can't you see what matters to me? I don't want to be programmed into something you think I should be; I want to discover who I am on my own!"*

CHAPTER THREE

I divorced barren reason from my bed.

Omar Khayyam

When I got to William and Mary College I took philosophy classes, hoping to learn more about what my life was about. While the ideas were interesting and the professors clever, there didn't seem to be anything that connected me with what my life felt like. Certainly, the philosophy professors' demeanor didn't suggest that they were in touch with the value of life in a way the rest of us weren't – in fact, they made an art out of holding life out at arm's length, perhaps so that no one could accuse them of being "subjective," which I gathered was a somewhat dirty word in that line of work. What I got from them were questions in answer to questions and a mental maze that was so much intellectual popcorn and hard to take seriously.

But that was not the case with one of my fellow students.

In the first semester of my sophomore year I was able to get into a philosophy seminar that had a limit of ten students. Unlike normal classes where the professors mostly talked at the students, it would be an opportunity for me to participate and openly explore my ideas. In the event, my ability to do that was limited because I was too self-conscious to open up, too anxious to show off what little knowledge I had. It was obvious that I was not the only one in that condition – we were, after all, sophomores.

But there was one student, Bill, who clearly stood apart. Bill was a lanky guy with a big nose that reminded me of no one so much as Ichabod Crane, but what truly distinguished him was that he was operating on a different level from the rest of us, not just intellectually, but emotionally. Far from showing off, he leaked his greater knowledge only as necessary, and his candid thoughtfulness was untainted by the reactions of others, including the professor. I secretly wished I could be more like him, but my insecurities were having none of that.

One morning about two-thirds of the way through the semester, we got the shocking news that Bill had committed suicide, had gone out on the cross-country course next to the campus and shot himself. I heard he left a note saying that he had come to realize from his study of philosophy that there was no God, and that being the case there was nothing left to live for. What Bill had not disclosed in the seminar was that he had come in as a devoutly religious young man, and was, in fact, a pre-divinity student.

When the seminar next met the professor opened the session by expressing regret, saying he would have tried to help if he had only known how "conflicted" Bill had been, then quickly moved on to the day's class material. I got the feeling, not just from the professor but from the rest of the college community, that Bill was regarded as a disturbed person whose fate was inevitable, a kind of roadkill on the intellectual highway, requiring a brief swerve and then speeding away.

I knew there was something wrong there, more than just the death of a human being, but I couldn't articulate it at the time, even to myself. I will try now: I certainly wasn't caught up in Christianity the way Bill was, but I identified with him because he was trying to answer the most important question of all, which is, "What makes life worth living?" – a question that can't be answered at arm's length.

What Bill and I shared was a need to feel the warmth of the inner most part of our being. In Bill's case that took the form of a nurturing God who stood for the value of loving and being loved. For me, it was an innate sense of the ultimate value of life that was so at odds with the mechanical, calculating parts of society that left me feeling out in the cold. And philosophy class was cold, handing life off to the mental maze that is the brain with its obscure explanations and ever finer distinctions.

I was somehow able to see that maze for what it was. But Bill, once he entered the maze, couldn't find his way out, and froze to death inside it.

CHAPTER FOUR

The pew is mightier than the pulpit.

Robert Ingersoll

Unlike Bill, I had not given up hope for a better life, yet I came out of my philosophy courses feeling that I had, at least for the time being, exhausted the possibilities for achieving some kind of reckoning with the value of my life. If I wasn't ready to figure out what my life was about on my own, the only thing to do was follow the blueprint that had been foisted on me by my father and my teachers in high school.

I would be a lawyer.

And the only thing I really needed out of college was a bachelor's degree so I could go to law school. In the event, there was a program under which I could skip the last year of undergraduate school and go directly to law school, thereby not wasting an unneeded year in college. At that point it seemed to me that the whole point of following the plan was to get there – the sooner the better.

By the time I was ready to go to law school, I was also ready to take another momentous step. Barbara was attractive, smart and just as immature and scared as I was. She felt safe. By marrying her I could check off the box on my resume that certified me as a card-carrying, red-blooded male and would not run the risk of looking foolish or failing romantically. That part of the program could be put to bed and I would be free to execute the rest of the plan.

The occasion of the wedding did, however, produce a troubling encounter with the issue of God. Barbara and I wanted a church wedding with a real pastor and, after the arrangements had been made, the reverend asked for a conference with the two of us. What we expected was a review of wedding details. What we got was a stern religious lecture, ending with his looking us in the eyes and demanding, as a *condition* of performing the wedding ceremony, that we acknowledge our belief in God and Jesus Christ as our savior. At that critical moment, Barbara and I glanced at each other and silently agreed that expediency was the order of the day.

I was sickened by how badly I felt telling that lie. While I told no one, including Barbara, about my reaction, it made me feel dirty inside to fake my identity to get married. And I wasn't just faking it to the pastor, I was confirming to Barbara that I was a faker.

Yet, I could have responded to the pastor's challenge by saying, "We appreciate your time and help up to this point, but, as much as we like the traditional Christian rituals that we've grown up with we are not Christians in the way that you are asking us to be. We'll get married somewhere else." – or words to that effect. That kind of moral courage could have washed over into our lives going forward, giving us a much better chance to be partners in all the ups and downs to come.

There is an irony about moral courage. It is, at once, among the most attractive, and the most difficult, of human qualities. Attractive, because it exhibits the unfettered creative energy that is the unique opportunity inherent in a human life, and difficult, because it requires ignoring all those voices in our heads insisting that it will lead to complication, rejection and danger. Those voices must have been in the brains of primitive humans whose best path to survival and reproductive success was risk management – stick to proven formulas and follow the tribal imperative. In our world, a different kind of success lies in just the opposite direction, where the courage to chart your own path energizes others to do the same, enabling a shared exploration and an interesting, vital life.

CHAPTER FIVE

The first thing we'll do is kill all the lawyers.

William Shakespeare

In the short term, the marriage left me more stable and focused than I'd ever been, and Barbara's almost immediate, unwanted pregnancy only added to my sense of urgency and purpose. Now we would have our children early and get that part of our lives done ahead of schedule. As for law school, I liked it. At last I was engaged in something that was really going to get me somewhere and, for the first time, I was a good student and actually studied – so much so that I got a scholarship after the first semester.

After our son Doug's birth, Barbara went back to work full-time, and I picked him up from daycare after classes and took care of him until she got home, when I usually went off to my job as a waiter. When Doug got meningitis at six months old (halfway through my second year of law school) and was in the hospital for three months, we handled it like real adults, even scrambling to cover the uninsured cost of brain surgery for him. I began to think that my fantasies of amounting to something in the world might not be entirely unrealistic.

Another transformation was taking place that I was less aware of: my notion of "amounting to something" was changing. While I had decided to be a lawyer early on, I had fixed on being a particular kind of lawyer. I had read the novel *Anatomy of a Murder*, and the protagonist in that story was my role model. A country lawyer who was a champion of the wrongly accused, eccentric but respected, the nemesis of interloper city lawyers, I would have my wood-paneled office near the county seat, my flyrod rigged in the corner and my shotgun hanging on the wall, both ready for spontaneous and frequent weekday sporting excursions. That was a life I could look forward to.

But I never got to try, because by the time I got to my second year of law school I had fallen under the sway of a different mentality. The competition for grades, then law review, and finally (the pot of gold at the end of the rainbow) a job with a prestigious big-city law firm with a fat starting salary and the promise of an even fatter partnership income seemed not just natural, but inevitable. The strongly prevailing view was that a smart young lawyer would be foolish to squander his talents on a country practice if he had the chance to make it to the big time. All of this was beyond my modest powers of resistance.

In the event, the dean of the law school sent me to Norfolk to interview with one of the best law firms in Virginia even before the normal recruiting season began and, despite my low expectations coming out of the interview, I was promptly offered a job at a startlingly high salary. Even my father was impressed. I was the come-out-of-nowhere hero of the family.

Of course, there would be no flyrod in the corner, no shotgun on the wall. I would work in the largest downtown office building and live in an apartment complex a few miles away. As an associate in a big-city law firm, I would work long hours in a ruthlessly competitive environment that left little time or energy for the other parts of my life.

I had been molded.

CHAPTER SIX

Fear is the first of man's natural enemies.

Carlos Castaneda

But first there was a bar to be cleared, and it was quite literally that – the bar exam. No matter what my law school credentials, I couldn't practice law without having passed the state- administered test. Because I was graduating from law school a semester early, I would not get the results of my exam, and therefore become a real lawyer, until I had been at my new job for two months. That meant I would begin my new job under a cloud – not a happy prospect, but there was no choice. Of course, most applicants passed the exam on the first try, and my new employers and professors thought it was not a worry.

But I worried. It wasn't that I thought I was likely to fail, but the idea that failure was even possible was too awful to contemplate – even a half-of-one-percent chance seemed like Russian roulette. So, I studied. I studied everything I could get my hands on about the bar exam when there was any time to do so. No need to ask where I was when President Kennedy was shot – I was studying for the bar exam. I hardly stopped to watch the news coverage.

The last month of law school passed quickly as I was distracted by the move to Norfolk. When I arrived at my new job, while everything was cordial and promising, one thing became quickly apparent. As an unlicensed lawyer, what I did was very different from what my contemporaries (competitors) did. I could not appear in court, even on the most minor procedural matters, could not prepare a final legal document, and most important of all, I could not advise clients. I was a research assistant and a go-for, somewhere between a lawyer and a secretary without the standing of either – a kind of non-person. With this humiliation my fears about the bar exam came back with redoubled force.

It was certainly conceivable that I had failed, and if so, I wouldn't be able to retake the exam for another six months. In that event, my employers might keep me on as a kind of half-lawyer in a state of limbo, now under the cloud of failure, in hopes I could redeem myself. Or they could simply treat me as a highly-touted imposter who could only be excised by euthanasia. The weight of these fears grew daily. Even if I wrote a good exam, what if my papers got switched with someone else's, a ne'er-do-well who didn't study at all? I hated that guy.

In fact, for the final few weeks before the results were due, I hated myself. I knew I had done everything possible to prepare for the exam, and that I was becoming seriously paranoid, but I couldn't let go of it. Scenes kept popping up in my head: the deadening shock of the first news of failure, facing the partners in the firm, telling Barbara, telling my father. No matter what I tried to do, these thoughts kept pushing themselves to the fore. Through leaden days and nightmarish nights, I fought to restore some sanity to my life, with little success. I was at war with my brain, and my brain was winning. During the last week of waiting I got almost no sleep and barely pretended to work – a zombie, only appearing to be alive. I told no one, not even Barbara, what I was feeling. It was hard enough admitting my weakness to myself. Defensive and irritable, I must have been a terrible husband and father.

When the day finally came, I got out of bed (no need to wake up), mechanically dressed myself, went to the office, closed the door, sat down in my chair and stared at the wall. The results were due to be published in the Norfolk afternoon paper, which came out about four o'clock. It was going to be a long day. And why couldn't the bar examiners find some less public, less humiliating way of delivering such awful news? At least when you find out you have terminal cancer, the doctor tells you in the privacy of his office.

Anticipating my doom, I passed the hours until about eleven o'clock, when Bernie Hall, the youngest of the partners, burst through the door and gaily asked if this wasn't the day the bar exam results were due.

I think the sound that came out of my parched mouth must have sounded something like "yes."

"Well," said he, "let's find out." I responded defensively that the paper didn't come out until four. "No problem," Bernie said as he reached for the phone with a carefree smile. "I know the secretary of the Virginia State Bar, and I'll call him in Richmond."

It was all I could do to keep from launching myself across the room, ripping the phone from Bernie's hand, and strangling him, at least until he was dead. Even a few more hours of my miserable life seemed incredibly precious.

The call didn't take long. Bernie got right through to the secretary, asked the question, and waited only a moment for the answer. He gave me a sorrowful look, shook his head, and then said, "You passed."

Shock, disbelief, and a new kind of numbness overtook me. I had so prepared myself for the worst, deadened myself down so powerfully, that I had no emotion left. I don't think I even smiled. When I got home, I sat down at the kitchen table and drank half a bottle of bourbon, virtually straight, but I couldn't get high, couldn't even feel the alcohol. After all that agony, there would be no celebration, no joy, not even relief, only a gradual decompression.

It is easy to be impressed by all the things our brains have done and continue to do for us. Their problem-solving abilities have created technologies that have transformed human experience, going from scratching around for survival to an astonishing level of comfort and safety.

Yet they are not just problem-solvers, but also problem-generators, futilely trying to solve the problem of an uncertain future, torturing their owners by sending them up blind alleys from which there seems to be no escape. While waiting for my bar exam results, I was in a torture chamber, just as unable to gain my freedom as if I had been chained to a stone wall in the cellar of a medieval castle.

CHAPTER SEVEN

An idle mind is the Devil's workshop.

Folk saying

In the weeks and months that followed, I became increasingly aware that the bar exam trauma was an extreme version of something that had been occurring since my early childhood. The accumulated doubts, fears and speculations in my brain formed a soggy overburden that damped down what could have otherwise been a smile on my face. Imagine my situation as being strapped in a chair in front of a computer monitor with my eyelids tapped open, going from screen to screen, every one bounded by banners, popups and crawls, reminding me of all the ways the world was not arranged the way I wanted it to be, how impotent I was in it *and how badly things could turn out*. Even if I didn't consciously focus on those boundaries, they were in my peripheral vision, dragging me down, inhibiting the best part of me.

Naturally, this took its toll emotionally, but I couldn't let it show at the office – that, after all, was where the game would be won or lost. What I do remember is that when I went home at the end of my workdays all I wanted was to be left alone. I think I must have been in that bar exam anxiety stupor, where I just dulled myself down to the point that nothing could get through – a kind of anxiety-ridden robot. I wanted my wife for what I wanted her for, and other than that I didn't want her or the children to make demands. I saw those intimate relationships much more in terms of problems than opportunities. And I had enough problems at the office.

Or at least it felt like I did. You wouldn't have known it from the way the partners and clients treated me. They acted as though I already knew what I was doing, and I did everything I could to encourage that notion. When the time came for my one-year review, the partner I reported to said that he had no criticism of my work – that as far as my bosses were concerned, I was doing everything right. I did not acknowledge then, or later, that I was scrambling to keep up, often bluffing my way through – better at looking good than doing good. That was the thing: I had to look good.

It seemed to work, at least on the outside. Clients started to come to me directly, bypassing the partners who would have been their normal point of contact, and the raises and bonuses from the firm were more than I would have dared ask for. In less than four years, I was made a partner in the firm, jumping ahead of all my contemporaries.

In a kind of role reversal, I was able to recruit my high school friend Larry to be a new associate in our firm. Larry had gone into the army for four years after undergraduate school, then to law school, after which he joined another firm in Norfolk for two years. Larry's firm was well-respected, but mine was particularly prestigious, representing many of the largest businesses and wealthiest people in town. I was able to persuade my partners, and then Larry, that having him join us would be a good move for all concerned.

At first, he did very well. His conscientiousness showed through in everything he did and, as always, he was eminently presentable. But after several years it became apparent that, in that fiercely competitive environment, good appearance and soldiering on were not enough. Larry did fine at the kinds of things that beginning lawyers do, but he was not someone who could move to the top.

For Larry, this was unbearable. He had done his level best to follow the plan the authorities in his life had laid out for him. Yet, no matter how hard he worked, no matter how conscientious he was, it wasn't enough. He became depressed, turning ever inward, not talking to anyone. Larry was a humane and even courageous person, but the one thing he didn't have the courage to do was to fall short.

I knew, Larry knew, everyone knew, that Larry was my guy, that I was his protector and I wanted to help him, but I didn't see how the trajectory I had helped to create could be reversed. For me, it was like watching someone die of cancer because of a toxic substance I had exposed them to.

He went to a psychiatrist, but it only got worse. After a year of this, Larry's wife called me one night after dinner. She was crying.

"Larry killed himself."

He had gone to his parents' house and, on the floor beside his mother's bed, he had knelt down and shot himself in the head with a pistol. No note, just dead.

It later occurred to me that Larry and my philosophy classmate Bill died of the same brain disease. Both lived in a programmed envelope that narrowly defined what made life worth living. Larry suffocated inside it. Bill approached his life more thoughtfully, but with the same result. Once the envelope fell away, he couldn't live outside it.

CHAPTER EIGHT

Man is a fool. He thinks his possessions make him secure.

Muhammad

Iremember my law practice years as a blur. I was everywhere, trying cases, wooing new clients, holding offices in the bar association, even taking charge of organizing the partners' meetings. There seemed to be no responsibility too large for the firm to give me, or for me to execute. I was the young lion, showing the way to the future. Barbara and I now had three children, all of whom were enrolled in private schools. We had built a big house on the water and owned a Buick the size of a small whale. I was checking those boxes off like there was no tomorrow. Was there nothing I couldn't do?

Well, yes.

For the first time, I was being exposed to the world of wealth, and I began to realize what that meant. Our firm represented many of the richest people in town, and in that culture one thing counted more than any other, and it wasn't character. The firm worked for some truly first-rate human beings who happened to be rich, but it also handled matters for some thoroughly unpleasant people who were still members of the club because they had wealth. Having money didn't just mean freedom or possessions, it also meant respectability, and even honor, if you were willing to give a little of it away to charity.

All of this was not lost on me. It was true that I was making a lot of money by any standard I had ever imagined, but I could see from how my senior partners were living that you couldn't get rich practicing law. Even the most successful lawyers worked long hours and lived modestly, at least compared to many of the entrepreneurs we represented. I had already gotten a taste of how easy it was to spend large amounts of current income so that it was gone without a trace. With that big house came a big mortgage and a big fire to feed. Watching how our clients worked, I came to understand that the way to get ahead financially was not to work for a business, but to own it. With that kind of quantum leap, you could transcend the cycle of ever- increasing income being matched by ever-increasing living expenses.

There was another problem. When I made the decision to go with a big-city commercial firm, I had tacitly made the decision to be a business functionary. That meant not only was I not saving anyone from the electric chair, jail, or even bankruptcy, but I also wasn't involved in people's lives in the kind of intimate, meaningful way I had imagined a country courthouse lawyer was. I was fungible – a replaceable cog in a big machine. What I did professionally was not likely to make a dramatic difference in anyone's life. I was working the margins. So, if I was going to be a part of the machine, why not get the payoff it could provide?

I began to plot.

It wasn't easy, because I had made myself the leader of the new generation of lawyers in the firm – the promoter of the future. How would the young lawyers I had helped to hire and encouraged feel when I abandoned ship?

While I struggled with this moral question, the issue was never in doubt. As it turned out, one of our more successful real estate developer clients, George Kaufman, was looking for a new partner, and I made sure he knew I was willing to be seduced. After a courtship dance of several months, we began serious negotiations that led to our forming a new real estate venture using his experience and money and my effort. We would build the first chain of all-suite hotels in the United States.

The idea was that a significant percentage of the traveling public needed longer-term accommodations, and a suite would be more like a temporary residence. Those long-stay guests could help us transcend the bane of commercial hotels – the "4/7 equation." Business travelers tend to leave home on Monday and return on Friday to be home with their families on the weekend (a four-night stay) with little revenue earned for the three nights of the weekend. But long-stay travelers usually stay right through weekends, providing a seven-day-per-week occupancy. Yet, despite the pervasiveness of all-suite hotels today, at the time, we seemed to be the only people who thought the concept made any sense. It would have been customary to get outside investors to fund most of the startup costs in such a venture, but despite a number of trips around the country to make presentations to raise money, we had no takers. Instead, we would have to rely on loans that both of us would be personally liable for, although all were based on George's personal assets.

Because equity contributions don't have to be paid back, but loans do, that meant an enormous increase in my personal financial exposure. Yet, I comforted myself by making a secret calculation. George was a high-profile person in the Norfolk community who had inherited wealth, married wealth, and made more. I figured that if our venture wasn't successful, he had the means to bail it and me out, and to not do so would damage his reputation in that community.

I also made a secret out of what I intended to do, with no one in the law firm being given any inkling of what was afoot. I even told Barbara as little as possible, and then it was more to inform than get assent. I was not interested in hearing dissenting opinions from anyone and I particularly didn't want to leak my plans prematurely, which could lead to all kinds of messy discussions and complications. My announcement would be a lightning stroke, presenting a done deal and forestalling all objections.

And so it was. When the time came to tell the other lawyers in the firm, I made sure to leave no room for discussion, steeling myself to the point that other people's feelings were not going to slow me down. To pull it off I made myself as cold as possible, hating myself the whole time.

Now the transition was complete. I had gone from wanting to be a country gentleman living close to nature, to becoming a big-city, bigtime, flying-around-the-country, cash-flowing entrepreneur. I wasn't excited about being a real estate developer, but I wanted the money, and that career seemed to be the path best calculated to get it. With that money I would have the means to get anything I wanted.

There was nothing wrong with being a real estate developer, or, for that matter, making money. The trouble was that the adding machine in my head was looking for the ultimate "bottom line," seeing money as a singular, future solution to everything that seemed to be missing in my life. It was as if I was looking at the world through a telescope, focused on a distant object, unable to see and experience the small, seemly inconsequential joys and excitements that were all around me and that are the very fabric of a happy life.

CHAPTER NINE

Every point of refuge has its price.

Linda Ronstadt

The beginning months of our hotel venture were not promising. We had bought an apartment complex in Atlanta and converted it into a hotel, which took longer and cost more than we expected. At the end of the first year, we had lost over a million dollars and I was personally liable for several times that amount in bank debt. Meanwhile, I was borrowing money to live on, since there was no income from which to pay salaries. Yet, by the end of the second year, the Atlanta operation became profitable, and with another hotel in Washington D.C. that was a success from the start, our business model began to take hold. Things were looking up at the office.

At home it was a different story.

Barbara had gone back to college part-time, and she was a lot more absorbed by her courses than she was by our home, our three children, or me. In fact, she was getting seriously depressed, almost incapable of domestic function, and the lack of sexual function was particularly wounding to me. For her sake as well as my own, I wanted to help her, but I didn't have the energy or the perspective to be of much use. In retrospect, I think I felt she had signed on to take care of the children and manage the household, and I had a hard time not only seeing her any other way but also seeing what I could do to make it work for her. For me she was a cornerstone of the structure I was trying to build in my life, and I needed her right there, holding up her end of the building – I was busy enough holding up my end.

We went to a psychiatrist, but that exercise only confirmed that things were very serious indeed in terms of her mental state and consequent disconnect from the children and me. Finally, an opportunity came for her to take a trip to Russia (she was a Russian language student) with a college-sponsored group. This at least was something she could get excited about, and even though it meant her being away from the children and me for three weeks I was desperate for anything that would revive her spirits.

That desperation manifested itself in another way. Before she left, I clearly implied to her that if she needed a relationship with another man to pull her out of her slump, she had my permission. At the time, I told myself that I was making the ultimate sacrifice for her happiness: acknowledging that if I couldn't make her happy she could find someone who could.

As soon as she stepped off the plane on her return, I knew something was very different. On the way home from the airport, she told me that she had had an affair with one of the tour directors – and wanted the affair to continue. It only added to my anguish that she was obviously relieved that she could want a man and enjoy it. At least I couldn't complain that she was dishonest.

Despite the fact that she had done precisely what I invited her to do, I was destroyed. However desperate I was for things to get better for Barbara, I was not prepared for this. She confirmed every insecurity I felt about myself. For fifteen years she had been crucial to my plan to make my life look right, and now that pretense was gone. What was also gone was my sense of responsibility toward her – at least now I could be free of someone whom I couldn't seem to help and who was no help to me.

She had fallen out of my programmed envelope.

CHAPTER TEN

People tend to eat the menu instead of the meal.

Aldous Huxley

We decided to separate. I would have custody of the children and she would go to school full-time. I would hire a nanny to keep the kids during the day and manage the household. I think I wanted to be a good parent. I know I wanted to *look* like a good parent. But the reality was that I was so self-absorbed, so frightened by Barbara's rejection of me, that I didn't have much energy left to engage the children, who were going through the trauma of having their parents separate. What my energy was focused on was my need to prove that I was a man – a sexual being.

In those days I was going around the country putting together deals to build hotels. Our latest effort was in Chicago, and I decided it would be my test site. I would go to a singles bar, pick up a woman, and do the deed or die trying. If I failed, at least no one I knew would witness my shame.

With advice from my local business contacts I picked out a bar and on the appointed night walked down the street to the place and looked inside. Groups of women sat at tables talking and laughing, just waiting to reject me. A feeling of abject depression came over me. I could not bring myself to reach for the door handle. I was stuck. I couldn't go in and I couldn't leave. I just stood there by the door pretending to wait for someone. I stood there a long time – the worst hour of my life – filled with dread and self-loathing. I had promised myself that I would go through with it, but it felt like death was waiting for me inside.

Finally, after an eternity, I forced myself to open the door and walked up to a table with three women, introduced myself, and sat down. I don't remember much after that – I was wolfing down the scotches – except that I zeroed in on the most likely-looking of the three and wound up in her apartment a few hours later. When we got in bed, she was not just willing; she showed a kind of enthusiasm for my body that I had never experienced in a woman. For my part, everything just worked. Not only had I not failed, it had been easy – ridiculously easy.

I left Chicago in a much better mood than the one in which I arrived. It must have shown, because on the flight back I sat in first class next to an attractive young lady who literally couldn't keep her hands off me. Her commitment to the friends she was visiting didn't keep her from detouring with me for an hour at the airport motel when we arrived.

Had I died and gone to heaven?

The next few months seemed to suggest that was the case. I had rented a house on the oceanfront at Virginia Beach, where there were a number of bars, like the one in Chicago, known for being one-night-stand merry-go-rounds. I hopped on. For a while, I was in a daze, like a kid dropped into his own candy store, unable to believe his luck. I had gotten what I had fantasized and obsessed about since my early teens – on-demand sex with girls who were both eager and pretty.

Yet, the daze didn't last. Over time, it all became increasingly unsatisfying, the sheer repetitiveness of it allowing me to see how empty it was. My brain had been pushing me to physically prove that I was an alpha male, and the repeated mechanical act of sex furnished that proof. I had knocked down a barrier that was blocking my path to further exploring what made life worth living. But heaven, it was not.

CHAPTER ELEVEN

All life is an experiment.

Oliver Wendell Holmes Jr.

Then I met Pat.

We met on the beach in front of my house, introduced by a woman who dated a man who worked for me. I later learned it was a setup, that this beautiful woman barely contained in a blue bikini had been dragged over to meet me by her friend who was urging her to get out of a problematical relationship with her boss. During our brief conversation on the beach she was not all that friendly (later she told me she didn't like being put on display), and I was relieved when our introducer called me that night and said that Pat would like to go out with me.

Our first date was dinner at the fanciest local restaurant, and she did most of the talking, telling me about her dreams and ambitions, conveying a sense of self-sufficiency and confidence about the future. Everything about her bearing and attitude belied the fact that she was a single mom, struggling to make ends meet and dealing with a very difficult personal situation. She was letting me know she had the courage to do whatever she needed to do, that even though she had been put on display she was not for sale.

We sat side by side at the table, so for much of the evening I was seeing her in profile, and I remember looking at her at one point and thinking that I had never been so close to such a beautiful woman. Later I realized that, for me, that moment was more than just a perception of physical beauty – it was an epiphany in which I was not just seeing a goddess but also seeing into the future, seeing the life we would have together and how she would open up heaven itself to me.

I had thought that over the last few months I had not only gained confidence but also some mastery over my feelings toward the opposite sex. But by the third date with Pat, I was caught in a whirlwind, having lost all sense of where the ground was. I was hopelessly in love, unable to think about anyone or anything else. That intoxication was to cost me dearly as we both disentangled ourselves from our past relationships. Pat was (and still is) beautiful and smart, with a rare gift for love and intimacy, topped off with a powerful personality – in other words, a dangerous woman. I had gone from being the driver of a Volkswagen Beetle to a passenger in a Ferrari and I wondered if I would ever get my hands on the steering wheel again.

But what a ride it was. I had never been around anyone so relentlessly engaged in life, and she was taking me with her. Before Pat, I hadn't truly listened to music. She could create a romantic atmosphere that made the music so real, I can still listen to the same music today and be transported back to that magical time. As for dancing, that bugaboo of my high school and college years, she simply wouldn't allow me *not* to dance. All my diffidence, embarrassment, and tenseness were straw in the wind to her will that I would discover what our bodies could do with music.

I knew how to *make* things happen – do deals, build buildings, create wealth – things that could be engineered to make a show in the future. Pat knew how to *let* life happen. She was spontaneous, open to every opportunity to create excitement, passion and fun – the very essence of present experience.

As soon as she disentangled herself from her relationship with her boss, which took the better part of a year, I asked her to marry me. She said yes and immediately embarked on planning a big wedding. In those days, outside of Hollywood, a second marriage was considered something to be celebrated quietly, if at all. I had some doubts about the very public nature of the thing, particularly given the fact that I had been separated from Barbara for less than two years. But I could not resist Pat's enthusiasm – hell, I couldn't resist her at all.

So, we had a big church wedding (two days after my divorce was final) with all our family and friends from our past lives. The reception was a drinking, dancing, laughing party, and Pat and I were the last to leave. A look at the forty-five-year-old wedding photographs reveals a beautiful, vivacious, relaxed bride and an incredulous groom with amazingly long sideburns.

I didn't make a decision to marry Pat in the way I had with Barbara. With Barbara, my brain had made a secret calculation. Like me, she was guarded and insecure, not a featured attraction to the opposite sex. Maybe I wouldn't disappoint her, and even if I did, perhaps she could at least settle for me. My brain had projected what was and was not possible for me, and charted a course that promised safety. But with Pat, there was no safety. It was self-evident that she was a powerful magnet, socially and sexually, and I had to believe that she had expectations *and desires* to match. This feeling was only confirmed by several of my male friends, who let me know that I was in over my head with a woman like that. Surely, I would fall short.

But by then there was something else at work in me. I had experienced, in full measure, the consequences of playing defense romantically, and I had to believe there was a better way. Even though I didn't see how I could win, I couldn't go back. I would push all my chips to the center of the table holding only a pair of deuces.

It was a leap of faith. I do not use that word in the sense that I took from its use in church, where I was told that if I believed in God, He would certainly make things right in a distant heaven. Instead, I would overrule my brain's future calculation and launch a present experiment.

CHAPTER TWELVE

Children should be seen and not heard.

Victorian saying

I had three children – Doug, Susan and Beth, aged fifteen, thirteen and ten – and Pat had a ten-year-old son, Ken, from her previous marriage. As for my children, I can't say that Barbara's and my divorce was the wrong thing for them. We were not breaking up a happy home. It was a plastic kind of thing that was kept looking good on the outside, but on the inside there was a mother who was so depressed she could hardly function and a father who was thoroughly frustrated and detached.

Barbara aside, what was wrong was the kind of parent I had been all along. That became all too apparent as I watched Pat shower love on Ken, which brought home to me and my children how differently I treated them. The double whammy of having a detached father and seeing how much better a parent *could be* left them angry – not only at me but also at Pat, despite her best efforts to bring together a new family.

It wasn't that I didn't care about the children, I just couldn't figure out how to deal with them. They were constantly doing things I didn't want them to do, asking for attention that I didn't know how to supply. Didn't they know how busy I was at the office? Didn't they know how scared I was that I wouldn't be able to pull the whole thing together?

You might say that I came by all of this honestly.

Since my early teens, I understood that my father would always support his family financially and maintain a respectable home environment, but I also sensed that he was a coward, insecure in his masculinity, obsessed with being embarrassed in any way, with a tendency to retreat into isolation under pressure – a frightened man who maintained an exterior gloss of confidence and control.

Dad really didn't trust anybody, including my mother. When my brothers and I were kids, the only time Mom went out at night was to PTA meetings at school, which Dad objected to. Once, when Mom had gone to one of these meetings against his will, she came home to find Dad and his domineering, nosy mother (who lived next door) waiting in the driveway to confront her for her disobedience. Mom was undeterred. It wasn't that she and Dad had horrible fights about these things – Dad would just sulk and get even more remote, and Mom would go on with her life. In the midst of that craziness, she refused to let Dad limit her life and refused to keep score even though she was carrying most of the burden.

I grew up thinking my mother had sacrificed her best years for my brothers and me because she was the one who assumed, not just all the parenting, but most of the effort required to maintain our physical environment. For more than twenty years we were the focus of her life, and my brothers and I were never in any doubt about it. Afterward, whenever she said she "loved every minute of it," I didn't believe her. How could anyone enjoy working sixteen-hour days, seven days a week, taking care of four troublesome boys and a demanding, remote husband?

Now I understand that she saw us as opportunities, not problems – saw the beauty in us, just as she saw the beauty in her flowerbeds, and had no trouble digging in the dirt to get to either one. Whatever was happening, she was present, in the moment, not keeping score and not judging.

When we complained about Dad's behavior, she would remind us that, "There's a lot of good in your father." As long as she had *that* husband and *those* children, she was *in there*, not just enduring, but *loving every minute of it.* More than any person I have ever known she modeled the reality that life isn't about the hand you're dealt, but how you play that hand.

So how was it that I imitated my father more than my mother?

I think the plan for success I had settled on as an impotent teenager was imbedded in that programmed envelope in my brain, to the point that carrying it out seemed existential, and everything else, including the children, became a sideshow. To the extent I did focus on them, I thought it was my duty to set limits and to structure their physical environment in a way that would make them turn out well. I conveniently assumed that my financial success would fund that environment.

If you had asked me at the time if I was trying to mold them, I would have denied it. But that is what it comes to.

CHAPTER THIRTEEN

What shall it profit a man
If he gain the whole world
And lose his own soul?

Jesus Christ

I was a financial success, at least temporarily. Eight years into our company, we had built twelve all-suite hotels, stretching from Washington D.C. to Austin Texas, and Pat and I were living high. We summered in Maine on our yacht, bought a waterfront farm as a weekend retreat, and stayed in the Hôtel Plaza Athénée in Paris.

Yet even though our business model was catching on in the marketplace, we were skating on thin ice. This was at the end of the Carter Administration, when interest rates were at historical highs, and building all those hotels required a lot of debt, much more than I thought made sense. But, as a minority partner, I didn't think I had any alternative but to go along with George's unlimited optimism. In fact, part of my secret calculation was that if I went along with his recklessness he'd feel even more dutybound to take financial responsibility for it. I now understand that as a result of that calculation, I surrendered my power to be a partner, to stand up for what I believed would be good, not only for me, but for George.

The result of all this was that, as they say in the financial world, we were highly leveraged, which is wonderful when things are getting better. But suddenly they got much worse. We had just built our two largest hotels in Houston when, in 1980, the oil market crashed. The Houston economy was built on oil, with the cycle of boom and bust that goes with that industry. We had invested in the boom and gotten the bust.

I had never liked the hotel business, but saw it as a way to make my life look right. Now I was realizing how much I could dislike it. When the economy of a city collapses, as Houston's did, you can't pick up your hotels and move them to a better place. In this situation, not only does occupancy go down, but hotels engage in the cannibalistic practice of cutting rates to lure other hotels customers so that even the units that are occupied produce much less revenue.

Suddenly we were losing three-quarters of a million dollars a month in Houston alone, more than wiping out our profits from all our other hotels. Worse, because we had just finished the largest of those Houston hotels, we had not qualified for permanent financing on it, so George and I were personally responsible for thirty million dollars of short-term construction debt with no way to pay it. At this point, George made it clear to me that when it came to paying my share of the debt, I was on my own. So much for my secret calculation.

In the middle of all this, I decided to buy another company that was losing money. The sailboat that Pat and I owned was built by the Hinckley Company, a famous old Maine yacht-building firm that had fallen on hard times after the death of the founder. I decided to team up with the founder's oldest son, Bob Hinckley, and buy the company. I would handle the business side and he would take care of sales.

So while I was trying to salvage a hotel company in crisis, I took on the turnaround of a bankrupt business that I knew almost nothing about and was seven hundred miles from home in a barely accessible part of Maine.

Not only that, the boat-building business itself is a notorious financial sinkhole.

Pat thought it was crazy.

Of course it was crazy, just like marrying her was crazy. Both were acts of passion with a life preserver nowhere in sight. I loved the beautiful sailboats they made at that boatyard nestled between the mountains and the cold green sea, and I loved the people who worked there and cared so much about building them as perfectly as they could. For the first time, I would be in a profession I loved – loved the boats, loved the place, loved the people. It was to be my first professional love affair – no secret calculation or financial endgame – but propelled by an invisible hand.

Still, the thing had to survive or there would be nothing left to love. So, I got the one hundred or so employees together and leveled with them about the condition of the company – something no one else had done to that point. Then I told them that everyone was taking a pay cut immediately to reduce expenses and that if and when we made money, the first profits would go to paying them back. I went to the banks and told them that they wouldn't like owning a boatyard and wrung concessions out of them to buy time. In my dealings with the company in those first days, all my efforts – with employees, banks and vendors – were built around conveying a true picture of utter, unvarnished reality. My behavior was not based on textbook learning, business experience, or even courage. I just didn't know what else to do.

Bob and I had to pump more cash in during the first year to keep a very leaky boat afloat, but after that things began to turn around. Bob produced the sales, and the people at the boatyard produced the boats. By the end of the second year we had made enough money, not only to pay back the cuts but also give all the employees a bonus. We were off and running.

Meanwhile, the hotel business continued to hemorrhage cash and I spent a lot of time in New York trying to sell it. Finally, after three years, I was able to sell my stock in the company – an enormous relief. I had gotten out from under millions of dollars of personally guaranteed debt and at last had some financial security.

I also had a great waterfront farm, a gorgeous yacht, a beautiful wife I was madly in love with, and four kids who were acting like they were going to make it through prep school and college. I had put a check in the "giving back" box by being on several charitable boards. On top of that, the company I was running was just famous enough to give me social cachet. I had the wealth, the respectability, and the personal relationships. I even had tons of free time since I only went to Maine one week a month, except for July and August, when I moved my family there – just like the rich people.

I had executed the plan.

CHAPTER FOURTEEN

It is enormous folly… when a man seeks, without faith, to be justified by outward works. Sometimes they even injure their brain, and extinguish nature, or, at least, make it useless.

Martin Luther, 1520

All I had to do was live my life.

That was turning out to be more difficult than I'd thought. All the pieces were in place, sure, but I was having trouble adapting to the new situation. For one thing, I had pictured the farm as a haven, just as my grandfather's farm was a haven to me when I was a child. But I wasn't that child anymore. My grandfather's farm was in a state of gentle bucolic decay by the time I knew it and I enjoyed it on those terms – it was mine to accept, but not alter.

Even though my farm was far more spectacular than my grandfather's, it seemed to me that it wanted all kinds of things: ponds to be built, roads to be improved, buildings to be renovated, wildlife habitat to be created – the list was endless. I couldn't stop seeing it as I wanted it to be rather than how it was. It was another project – another problem to be solved.

It was amazing how much anxiety I could generate over the outcome of my efforts. Before, I had thought my obsessiveness stemmed from having so much at risk. Now, my paranoia about the future seemed to have taken on a life of its own, independent of the stakes.

That wasn't all. If I was able to suspend my fixation on the future and just focus on relaxing at the farm, doing all the things I had fantasized about, such as fishing, hunting or sailing, I became antsy and, after a short while, depressed.

I had gotten to heaven and it wasn't there.

It wasn't just at the farm, either. With our newfound freedom, Pat and I decided to take the vacation to end all vacations. We discovered a small South Seas island near Fiji that had a luxury resort consisting of only four separated beach cottages with every service and amenity provided in such a way that we didn't even have to see any other guest if we didn't want to. My sexy young wife and I would have a tropical island to ourselves, with none of the hassles of being deserted and away from any crass distractions or worldly cares.

When we got there for our six weeks' vacation, it lived up to its advance billing. It was utterly idyllic, with pristine white beaches, waving palms, lush flowers and perfect climate – the most inviting place I'd ever seen. The food served in our cabin was delicious, and fishing, snorkeling and any other conceivable activity was available on demand, with or without guides. It was perfect.

At least it was for a few days. Then the headaches started. They would begin shortly after I woke up in the morning and stay with me all day. Until that time, I probably hadn't had five headaches in my life, so the experience was both mystifying and worrying. I took the usual remedies, to no avail. After a week with no relief, we flew to Fiji to see a doctor, who could find no apparent cause for my pain. We went back to the island, but it was no use – the headaches wouldn't go away. Because I was so uncomfortable, neither of us were having any fun, so we decided to go home where I could get more effective medical help, or at least suffer at less expense. The day we arrived in the United States the headaches stopped, never to return.

My brain couldn't stand unemployment, couldn't deal with accepting a happy present in which there was no future result to be engineered, so it sabotaged my body.

CHAPTER FIFTEEN

Enlightenment is the intentional stopping of the spontaneous
activity of the mind stuff.

Patanjali, 400 CE

I decided to try Zen meditation.

Zen is based around the idea of quieting your conscious mind, getting
it out of the way, so that you can live in the present, unhindered by the
past or the future, and thus fully appreciate present human existence.
The idea is that continuous meditation will wash over into everyday
experience in a way that keeps the meanderings of the conscious mind
from polluting your life. That sounded good to me.

I read several primers on Zen and began to experiment with sitting
meditation (zazen) at home. In those sitting sessions, usually lasting
forty-five minutes, I tried, as instructed by my books, to just observe my
thoughts, letting them pass by without judging them, with the goal of
letting them run out of steam. Just as predicted by the books, my brain
kept throwing thoughts up, resisting any effort to get it to settle down
and take a break. It wasn't only that meditation required considerable
effort and discipline, but there was something inside me that was actively
fighting it. That something was so cunning and subtle that I sometimes
personified it as an elusive demon that didn't want me to have a life.

After some months of this, I decided I needed some help. A friend who had been a practicing Zen student for many years suggested I go to a Zen monastery where I could meditate in a more structured environment and get some guidance. This was a serious escalation in my spiritual/ psychological search because it required a commitment to both time and travel since nothing nearby seemed suitable. More importantly, it required temporary residence at a monastery, with all its rigors and disciplines. These places are not country clubs. They are modeled around traditional religious monasteries, which emphasize communal living, austerity, and silence. A student in residence is expected to be meditating, working (kitchen duty, housecleaning, or yard work), eating (at precisely scheduled times), listening to Zen lectures, or sleeping – a far cry from the Plaza Athénée.

The staff at the monastery is not only there to teach but also to enforce the strict pattern of behavior thought to be conducive to effective meditation – simplicity, silence and refraining from all frivolity. Part of the idea is to eliminate the need for thinking so the student can begin to realize that the spontaneous speculations and ramblings of the conscious mind (which continue in the absence of any need or stimulation) have a life of their own, which is no life at all.

The first monastery I went to (Rochester Zen Center) put considerable emphasis on achieving a truly mindless state (satori), which was said to be the culmination of the meditation process in which the student sees, in a flash of white light, the true nature of reality. I certainly had no objection to white light, but the prospect of attaining satori didn't interest me that much. I just wanted that unruly brain of mine to settle down.

My time at the Rochester Center, two times totaling ten days, was built around a voluntary meditation schedule, and even though I meditated more than I did at home, I could pace myself and stop when I wanted to. I didn't feel I'd made much progress while I was there, and after my last session, I was left feeling that any chance of taming my brain would require a much more rigorous effort.

This time I signed on for a seven-day intensive meditation retreat at Zen Mountain Monastery in rural New York that *required* eight to nine hours of sitting meditation a day beginning at 5:30 a.m. and ending at 9:00 p.m. The breaks in the meditation schedule were mostly for kitchen and yard work, Zen lectures and meals. All of this was done in utter silence and according to a precise schedule in which tardiness was neither appreciated nor condoned. At the meditation sessions, roving monitors went up and down the line of sitting students with a bamboo cane, and anyone caught sleeping, or even moving, got a whack across the back, which could be heard throughout the room.

From the first moment I sat down to meditate at the sesshin, I knew this time was going to be different. My brain panicked at the idea that I had committed myself to this insane regimen. Whereas before I had trouble slowing my brain down, now I experienced an incredibly accelerated level of mental activity in which my mind was challenging me head-on. It was as if someone had loaded every conceivable thought I could have into a machine gun and fired them at me in random, rapid order.

Unfortunately, that wasn't all. I was in pain – serious physical pain. After a few hours of sitting in the cross-legged position on that cushion, my knees and ankles hurt excruciatingly. I told myself that because I was twice the age of most of the people in the room and therefore less flexible; it was unfair. I plotted to sneak out and buy massive doses of Motrin to blot out the pain. I silently raged at the teachers, whose severe aspect warned that they would cut me no slack, and at the other students, whose peer pressure kept me sitting there in agony. Over the week my mental image of my car became more and more beautiful because it was what would take me from that damned place.

Zen lectures were given every day, but unfortunately we heard them in the dreaded cross-legged position. To the extent I could focus on them, they had themes that seemed familiar from my Zen reading, but my mind and body were in no shape to receive new information, much less inspiration. It was one long torture session.

At the end of the last day of the retreat, the students finally got to talk to each other and the teachers. When I described my experience to the teachers and seasoned students, I was told I should not be discouraged. It was not unusual and should be regarded as a step in the process.

Certainly, I knew in advance that Zen meditation was no quick, easy fix for anything, and I didn't want to be a coward in the face of pain and frustration if there was something valuable to be learned. But my time with experienced students did not leave me feeling encouraged. Simply put, I didn't get the feeling they were where I wanted to be. When the retreat was over, I drove away with an enormous sense of relief, relief it was over and relief that I had no commitment to ever sit cross-legged on a cushion again – and I didn't.

But the experience did bring into sharper focus the utter outrage my brain was committing on my person. The frantic mental activity never slowed down during seven days of attempted meditation. Why would I do this to me? Why would my brain make the exercise necessary at all and then fight the process so vengefully? I did not want it. I did not intend it. So how did it happen?

All I could think was that it happened the same way my bar exam trauma, my inability to enjoy the farm and my failed vacation happened. The difference now was that I had confronted the issue of my runaway brain head-on. Before, when I faced the problem, I could default to my accustomed pattern of frantic external activity, thereby deflecting my brain's unwanted excursions into a glancing blow – something I could put off for future resolution.

But now there was no future. That frantic activity was built around getting things –possessions, status, relationships – and I had everything I knew to want. The only thing I was after now was the ability to enjoy what I already had. But the brain I had used to engineer the acquisition of all those things was no help in achieving that goal. Far from helping, it had gone into open revolt.

CHAPTER SIXTEEN

Mythology is somebody else's religion.

Joseph Campbell

A few months after I got back from the retreat, my older daughter Susan gave me a videotaped series of PBS programs featuring Joseph Campbell, a leading authority on mythology and self-confessed maverick in the world of religion.

I was smitten from the first tape. For one thing, he threw a hand grenade right into the middle of the Christianity that so baffled me as a child. He was blunt about the inhumanity of the notion that there could one chosen people, one religion, and that all who did not follow it were doomed. More importantly, he said the thrust of most mythologies – religions – was to put its followers *in accord* with the world around them and their own bodies, to help them to feel that the world was not flawed and evil but good and right, and to help them to feel that their natural impulses were to be enhanced and vivified, not judged and suppressed. He explained that despite its prominence in the last two thousand years, viewed against the long sweep of mythological history, Christianity was at an extreme, with its emphasis on original sin and judging unworthy humanity at the end of time.

I didn't need Campbell to convince me that the miraculous stories in the Bible hadn't happened, but he added that those stories were strikingly similar to stories which existed in other mythologies all over the world – mythologies that existed both before and after biblical times. Stories of immaculate conceptions, deaths and resurrections, global floods, and people being swallowed by whales (or fish) abounded in totally disconnected cultures, including those of native (North and South) Americans. The story of Moses is so similar to an earlier legend that the biblical author of that tale would probably be charged with copyright infringement under modern law.

Campbell also helped me see that there was something worthwhile for me in mythological stories. A central thrust of his work is that the universality of these stories shows they are not to be taken as historical facts but as directional signs pointing toward the valuable and immutable part of human existence. So, for example, the notion of immaculate conception is a metaphor for the idea that the essence of humanity does not originate with biology or any other mechanical process but comes from a place that can be known only to the heart and never to the rational mind.

This was eye-opening stuff. For the first time, I was able to gain some perspective on *what religion was.*

One of the stories Campbell zeroed in on was the fire-breathing dragon in the cave, defending his gold and his beautiful virgin captive from the onslaught of the brave knight. To his way of thinking, the story wasn't about the lizard out there, but the lizard in you; that the dragon represented the part of your brain that just wanted to grasp and possess and that the knight was your humanity struggling to overcome that reptilian, venal force. When Campbell said that the dragon had the gold and the beautiful girl but couldn't do anything with either one, I couldn't help but think about my failed South Seas vacation with Pat.

Campbell also ripped apart my limited notion of what the word "God" could mean. Campbell said that in most mythologies, gods that looked and acted like people (anthropomorphic gods) were considered to be tribal manifestations of a larger universal force that defied any description. What I took from Campbell was that God wasn't a person or anything like a person – didn't have plans or intentions, didn't take sides or get mad. And what happened down here on Earth actually mattered – God wasn't just playing cosmic solitaire. He didn't have a brain, but transcended thinking altogether. Campbell summarized all this by saying that "God" is just the ultimate word for transcendence. After thinking about this, I realized that my alienation from the God of my childhood didn't mean I had to give up on *God*.

What Campbell said sounded right to the point of being obvious. It wasn't just intellectual stimulation; I was encouraged about how to think about my life. I won't say that it was the white light of satori, but it opened me up to the possibility that I could go beyond traditional formulas and imagery in thinking about the value of my existence.

I say opened me up to the possibility because he offered no path for realizing my potential as a human being other than to find some new, more appropriate mythology, offering no suggestion as to what that mythology would be in the modern world. All he would say is that mythologies cannot be predicted because they come from the same place that dreams do and are therefore unbidden – and that any mythology now must encompass the whole world because of the global nature of the human community created by communication technology.

In thinking about this, I had a hard time figuring out how a modern mythology might even work, because all the mythologies I knew about relied on stories about supernatural occurrences to get to the transcendent quality of life. Would modern, scientifically-oriented minds stand still for this? I didn't think mine would.

CHAPTER SEVENTEEN

The brain is a biological gadget.

Stephen Pinker

My interest in Campbell drove me to investigate the attitude of the academic world toward this person who seemed to be not just a maverick, but my kind of maverick. Since I was friends with the president of St. Mary's College of Maryland across the river from my farm, I asked her if she could introduce me to someone in their religion department with whom I could discuss this. She professed some interest in taking part in the discussion herself and arranged a lunch with the head of the religion department.

In the event, the three of us didn't spend much time talking about Joseph Campbell, who was dismissed with a wave of the professor's hand, and the conversation quickly turned to a general discussion of religion in the modern world. As I listened to an analysis of several of the finer points of religious theory, I began to realize that these people's interest in the subject came from an entirely different place than mine. Like my college philosophy professors, their focus was on religion only as a cultural phenomenon to be studied, analyzed and put into perspective, but always kept at arm's length. When I made a feeble attempt to bring the discussion into the realm of the transcendent, I think they were actually a little put off, as if I had mentioned that I had forgotten to wash my underwear.

Here I was, the heathen Christian apostate, feeling confused and maybe even a little hurt that they had summarily dismissed the subject that was of such profound and consuming interest to me – *God*.

After lunch, when my college president friend and I went back to her office to continue our discussion without the professor, I bravely brought up the subject of *God* again. She explained that in her younger years she had been an ardent practicing Christian but abandoned all that and came to the conclusion that the rational was all there was. With that, she reached up to her bookshelf, pulled down a book, and casually shoved it across the table, saying, "This is what I believe." The book was *How the Mind Works* by Steven Pinker, a professor of psychology specializing in cognitive neuroscience, then at MIT.

I went home and started reading – and I kept reading. The book wasn't just interesting; it was fun. Pinker is an exponent of several new and somewhat controversial branches of science: evolutionary psychology and the computational theory of the mind. Pinker describes the key ideas in the beginning of the book: "The mind is a system of organs of computation, designed by natural selection to solve the kinds of problems our ancestors faced in their foraging way of life, in particular, understanding and outmaneuvering objects, animals, plants, and other people." His discussion of computer-controlled robots that attempt to ape human capabilities helped me visualize my own brain.

Pinker runs the gamut from technical explanations of how computational devices (computers) work to detailing how modern humans' excessive desire for sugar and fats is a carryover from the desperate need to build body fat in our hunter/gatherer ancestors, to describing how women preferring rich men in the modern world relates to the biologically successful strategy of primitive women wanting to mate with male overachievers. To my sensibilities, Pinker is ruthlessly clearheaded, and even his most technical discussions are leavened with humor and an extraordinary amount of common sense. He is also a master at erudition – turning to superficially unrelated subjects to illuminate the point at hand.

Most of the book is given over to the mechanics of the mind – its origins, functions, and the results it produces. But nuggets sprinkled throughout show that Pinker doesn't think that the world is all mechanics. Some examples:

> A human being is simultaneously a machine and a sentient free agent…the mechanistic stance allows us to understand what makes us tick and how we fit into the physical universe. When those discussions wind down for the day, we go back to talking about each other as free and dignified human beings.

Another:

> Given that the mind is a product of natural selection, it should not have the miraculous ability to commune with all truths; it should have the mere ability to solve problems that are sufficiently similar to the mundane survival challenges of our ancestors. According to a saying, if you give a boy a hammer, the whole world becomes a nail. If you give a species an elementary grasp of mechanics, biology and psychology, the whole world becomes a machine, a jungle, and a society. I will suggest that religion and philosophy are in part the application of mental tools to problems they were not designed to solve.

The book ends with Pinker explaining an idea he calls "Cognitive Closure," summarized by these words from the final chapter:

> We are organisms, not angels, and our minds are organs, not pipelines to the truth. Our minds evolved by natural selection

to solve the problems that were life-and-death matters to our ancestors…not to answer any question we are capable of asking.

Pinker articulates, in eloquent fashion, ideas that had been simmering on the edge of my consciousness, using words that brought those ideas into sharper focus. My brain was a "machine" designed to win in a "jungle." I was not a "robot" but a "free and dignified human being." And I didn't have to reject science, but see it as a limited tool, just as my brain is a limited tool.

CHAPTER EIGHTEEN

Computers are like Old Testament gods; lots of rules
and no mercy.

Joseph Campbell

Pinker's book was intriguing, but it took another event to bring home what all this was about for me.

I got a personal computer.

Astonishingly, it went very well. I bought a laptop, signed on with a service provider, and taught myself how to type using a typing tutorial program, all within the space of a month. Email was a revelation to me, and for the first time in my life I became a good correspondent. In the purely mechanical process of sending electronic mail, the computer was straightforward, easy to use and reasonably reliable.

However, when I tried to use the more complex functions of the machine, I found it frustrating. It was a thinking machine, sure, but one that was absolutely uncompromising in its demand for exactness on its terms.

I never knew the meaning of the phrase "literal-minded" until I used the computer. In typing an address or giving an instruction through one of the menus it had to be *precisely* right or it was nothing doing. Even putting a space in the wrong place was fatal to a webpage address.

When I tried to get it to execute an instruction, I found it was totally unforgiving, doing exactly what it had been programmed to do and nothing more and nothing less. If I asked it to do something without understanding the scope of the instruction I had given, it would, like the broom in the "Sorcerer's Apprentice," carry out that instruction forever, whether or not it made any sense.

The people who programmed the thing knew they had to avoid ambiguity, so they broke down the instructions as much as possible, which meant that the menus were encyclopedic – overwhelmingly so. Even then, the organization of the menus was beyond cryptic – the way to initiate the stop sequence was to click on Start. The problem was that the computer knew only black and white, straight lines, and right-angled corners – no shades of gray, no curves. If my idea of how to describe or do something was different from the computer's, there was no negotiation, no compromise – I did it the computer's way or not at all. When I went to a web address to find a specific piece of information, often the problem wasn't too little information but too much, and I would have to sort through hundreds of choices to find what I wanted. The problem was that the thing had no focus or, at the very least, not my focus. Didn't it know what I was looking for? Then there were times the machine would unceremoniously decide that it had had enough and opt out altogether, either by issuing a cryptic announcement like "This Program Has Executed An Illegal Operation And Will Be Shut Down" or by simply locking up and ceasing to function. This seemed to occur when I needed the thing the most.

Of course, the computer is only a machine, a technological tool, but I couldn't help but view it as a thinking machine – one that was intent on its own plan and no other, that would do things in its own way whether it served my interests or not, that would keep doing something even when I wanted it to stop, that would flood me with every kind of information except what I needed.

Like my brain.

I decided to find out how computers worked. I already knew a computer science professor, so I asked for his recommendation on some basic books on the subject. Between the reading and some follow-up help from the professor, I discovered that although modern computers can store and process enormous amounts of information, the basics of how they work is pretty simple.

I learned that in order for a computer to work, two things are necessary – algorithms and an organized database. An algorithm is a formula – *if this, then that*. The database is a catalogue of information. Stated another way, the algorithm is the recipe and the database the pantry of ingredients. The algorithm for a cake: Combine one pound of flour, two eggs, one cup of sugar, one tablespoon of baking powder and a pinch of salt, mix in a bowl, put the mixture in a baking pan and bake at three hundred seventy-five degrees for forty minutes. The "organized" part of the database is that the algorithm has to know where to find the flour, eggs, et cetera in the pantry. All of this, of course, can't be done without hardware – bowls, pans, stove – and a human being to move them around.

Then there is the issue of "machine architecture" – the pots and pans and their arrangement and use. Modern computers use the binary system, which employs the symbols "0" and "1" as the building blocks ("bits") for its operations and these symbols represent true (1) and false (0). These true/false indications, which are represented by different voltage levels, implement the algorithmic process – Is it sugar or not? Is it three hundred seventy-five degrees or not? – and lead to the ultimate terminating process – Is it a cake or not?

Each of these true/false calls has a lengthy subset of true/false decisions to make – Is the oven door opened or closed? Is the tablespoon of baking powder rounded or flat? – and so on. It is not enough to say "sugar" – is it granulated or powdered? Anal precision is at the heart of computers.

CHAPTER NINETEEN

Man has no time to be anything but a machine.

Henry Thoreau

Having learned something about inanimate computers, I began to do some reading on the makeup and function of the human brain with a view to getting a sense of how knowing about the former might help understanding the latter.

Not surprisingly, a lot more is known about the PC than the human brain – after all, humans designed the PC and evolution designed the brain. At the same time, a great body of widely-accepted knowledge has been gained about the brain in the last one hundred years or so, and from my reading it became quickly clear that the human brain fits the definition of a computer: it employs an organized database and algorithms to solve problems. Both employ an on/off methodology to transmit information. In the case of the PC it is a gate open or closed, and in the case of the brain it is the spike or no spike of a neuron. Neuroscientists refer to this spike or no spike mechanism as the "all or nothing" principle. Both employ flip-flop circuits to derive a single output from multiple inputs. That is the fundamental process, whether it's finding a specific piece of information on a website or aiming a spear to intercept the path of a fleeing animal.

There are, obviously, fundamental differences as well. The PC's programming is fixed and can only be changed by an external agent, but the brain can modify its software and hardware internally to adapt to the experience of its owner. The brain is immensely more powerful, being able to process many times more bits of information. The PC can only do one thing at time, while the brain can do many things at once. While I am writing these words, my brain is regulating my heartbeat and respiration (along with dozens of other "housekeeping" functions in my body) as well as processing words and ideas and activating my fingers on the keyboard.

The brain is also slow, at least compared to the PC, in terms of the rate at which it processes information. This is because it relies principally on chemical changes to transmit and process information, whereas the PC relies exclusively on electricity, which travels at the speed of light, and because the brain simultaneously divides its power up among many different functions.

Thinking about all this information, it was hard for me not to conclude that while brains and PCs are very different as to origin and physical characteristics, they are very similar as to process and function. They both try to do similar things, just with different hardware. Of course, the idea of brain as a computer is not new and has been discussed since computers were first developed. Most of that discussion has been centered on how capable and powerful the biological machine is. What I was coming to realize is how limited it is, and how those limits interfered with what I ultimately wanted out of life.

Those limits were summed up in several fundamental principles laid out in my computer science textbook:

The level of intelligence displayed by machines is limited by the intelligence that can be conveyed through algorithms. If no algorithm exists for performing a task, then that task lies beyond the capabilities of machines.

The value of my life was not to be found in future *results*, but in present *experience*. Yet the thing in my head – the filter through which I saw the world – was designed to project results, always looking for certainty.

Once an algorithm for performing a task has been found, the performance of that task no longer requires an understanding of the principles on which the algorithm is based.

Instinct is another word for imbedded programming. It is not just residual programming from the ancient past – say, regarding reproductive success as existential – but also more recent programming, when during my early life I unconsciously constructed a soul-numbing strategy for dealing with life as I found it then. In both cases this programming overruled my ability to choose how I wanted to be in the present. I was a robot without knowing why.

[In] Computer Science...a line is drawn between processes that culminate with an answer and those that merely proceed forever without producing a result.

For primitive humans there was only one answer that ultimately counted – winning in that ruthless evolutionary contest in which good was never good enough, competitors constantly upping the level of their game. The trouble was that, for me, good *was* never good enough. Lord knows, I was spending a lot of time in that place, comparing my failings and achievements with other peoples', lurching between elation and despair. It wasn't just that I was afraid that I might not measure up, but that my solitary thought process was dominated by endless, unsatisfying comparisons.

Each step in an algorithm does not require creative skills. Rather, it requires only the ability to follow directions.

Algorithmic is just another word for mechanical – the seeming inevitability of cause and effect. Good science captures that inevitability through measurement and prediction. But that inevitability was not good for *me*. I didn't want to be locked into an inevitable result, but open to possibilities. Of course, I needed comparison and projection to structure my safety and comfort, but that could only be a launching pad for *creating* my life.

Joseph Campbell and Stephen Pinker had helped me to appreciate that there was a me that was not my brain. Yet that appreciation, by itself, was still at arm's length – something that could be taught in philosophy class. But with these computer principles I could go beyond the intellectual to the experiential, linking the ongoing useless drama in my head with the workings of a mechanical tool that was constantly letting me know how limited and perverse it was. That allowed me to see it as a limited machine, separate from unlimited me. More specifically, I saw the opportunity to treat my brain the way I do my personal computer, using the features that help me and avoiding those that leave me confused and alienated.

Now I had a trail of breadcrumbs to follow in my quest to break through the barrier between me and the better life I so desperately wanted.

CHAPTER TWENTY

If you can meet with triumph and disaster
And treat those two imposters just the same...

Rudyard Kipling

After eight years of owning the Hinckley Company, things had settled into routine. We were selling around fifteen sailboats a year and producing a modest profit. I continued to love the place and the people, although I had to admit that the boats themselves had become more business than pleasure, and businesses have no end of problems. I was also struggling to find a way to grow a business that was confined to a narrow niche market. And then, suddenly, the issue became not growth, but survival.

In 1990, Congress made a major revision of the tax code, including a proviso that put an excise tax (think sales tax) of ten percent on certain luxuries, among which were pleasure boats costing over fifty thousand dollars. Even though the provision would add little to government revenues, it was intended to show the government was serious about "fairness" in distributing the tax burden. In the event, what was serious was the impact on yacht-building companies and their thousands of workers. Our customer base regarded the tax as punitive and "unfair," and they either stopped buying yachts altogether or went to another country to do so. Almost overnight, our sales went to zero and we were facing a brick wall. How do you have a boat company if you can't sell boats?

Yet, even though things looked hopeless, we had to do *something*. The first steps were to eliminate every expense possible, including Bob's and my salaries, and to make major employee layoffs. But that would only limit losses, and we needed to find a way to produce income. The only thing we could think of was to develop an international pool of customers who would not be subject to the tax, not an easy thing to do on short notice.

It helped that while Hinckley didn't have many foreign customers, it did have an international reputation for quality and beauty, and I would need to ride that reputation pretty hard. It also helped that Japan's economy was booming and wealthy individuals there had the appetite and means to purchase prestigious luxury products. So, while we saw some opportunities in Western Europe, our main focus was on Japan.

Thanks to our reputation, I was quickly able to forge a relationship with a trading partner in the form of Sumitomo – one of the largest industrial conglomerates in Japan – which opened many doors. What also opened was my eyes to an entirely different culture. I had grown up in the aftermath of World War II, and as the notion of "yellow peril" was fresh in my mind I wasn't sure what to expect.

What I found was a charming culture that took mutual respect to levels unimaginable to Western sensibilities. In the US, an exchange of business cards is an afterthought, casually tossed across the conference table at some point in the meeting. In Japan, that exchange occurs at the time of introduction, when time slows down as each party carefully takes their card out and hands it to the other party, who receives it respectfully and carefully examines it as if it was a precious object. What a way to begin a relationship!

Every time I arrived in Japan for a visit, the first night would be devoted to a welcoming dinner, at which I would be treated to a choreographed meal with a number of Sumitomo executives, served by women in traditional Japanese dress. At the beginning of these dinners, everyone was extremely deferential to me, but by the end they were all so drunk I might as well not have been in the room. That was charming too.

My counterpart at Sumitomo was a man named Maruka, and we quickly formed a close friendship, based in no small part on our shared sense of humor about our respective cultures. He was particularly fond of plays on words. Because the Japanese expression for "good morning" sounds like "Ohio," whenever I would first see him in the morning, he would always say, "Indiana." As we traveled Japan together, I realized how narrowly I had pictured what a happy society would have to be. And when Maruka visited me in the US, I came to the humbling realization that he knew as much about my country as I did.

Back at home, I was pulled into the effort to repeal the luxury tax. Not only was Hinckley one of the highest-profile companies in one of the largest boatbuilding states, but the US Senate Majority Leader George Mitchell was one of Maine's senators. I got together with other boat-builders in Maine and we called on the senator, explaining the severe impact on Maine's blue-collar workers and the nonexistent impact on the wealthy. I think he got it right away, but since he'd had a hand in crafting the tax revision, including the excise tax, he was in an awkward position. Still, he introduced me to other senators to whom I was able to make our case.

The result was that I became one of the leading lobbyists for repeal of the tax, spending a lot of time in Washington in private meetings with congressmen, testifying before a senate committee, and writing an editorial that ran in many newspapers across the country, including *The Washington Post*.

It quickly became clear that there was no viable argument against repeal since the income tax on lost wages in the boating industry was many times the small amount of excise tax collected. A year into the tax, we were able to get the senate to pass a *unanimous* resolution calling for repeal, but it took another year to get the whole thing through Congress. In the meantime, our company was scraping by in shrunken form, living on a small number of foreign sales, barely keeping our nose above water. But we got through it, quickly reviving on the pent-up demand once the tax went away, and were able to hire back most of our laid-off employees.

I wouldn't wish that whole experience on those laid-off employees, but I'm glad I didn't miss it. I absorbed an appreciation of other cultures, had a fascinating inside look at national politics, and got to spend time with many interesting, smart people. I had fun.

As was the case with the end of my first marriage, something I was deathly afraid of turned out to be good for me, reminding me that my life is not about closing in on my brain's projections, but opening up to the uncertainty of present experience.

CHAPTER TWENTY-ONE

You better not cry
Better not pout
I'm telling you why
Santa Claus is coming to town.

John Frederick Coots and Haven Gillespie

For a number of years after we moved to the farm our next-door neighbors held a Christmas Eve party to which they would invite friends with small children. The highlight of the evening, timed to occur just before the children were ready to fall asleep, was the appearance of Santa Claus, who would give them presents and listen to their Christmas wishes. One year, to Pat's delight, they invited me to play Santa.

I, on the other hand, was not delighted. The idea of being an actor held no appeal to me – plus, I had a particular problem picturing myself as the roly-poly icon of all things Christmas and serious doubts about my ability to bring it off. I could only too vividly picture my embarrassment when the children were unconvinced. Besides, I had my dignity to think about.

Pat was having none of it. She said that it was an incredible opportunity for the children and me and I would make a great Santa, whereupon she went down to our neighbors' and picked up the Santa costume.

Meanwhile, I wasn't budging, having decided that this time she was not going to steamroll me into something I felt uncomfortable about.

But steamrolled I was. She was too smart to argue about it, knowing that I would just dig my heels in and create a stalemate. Rather, she pleaded with me in a way that only a beautiful woman can, cajoling, wheedling – begging even – with slightly suggestive caresses and that killer smile of hers. Before I knew it, I was stuffing a pillow under my red jacket and trying on a white beard.

Christmas Eve, I put the outfit on for the actual performance and began to get into the spirit of the thing, in spite of my reluctance, thanks in no small part to the praise and encouragement of a dozen or so other family members who had gathered at the farm for the season. We had arranged for our son Ken to drive me the half-mile to our neighbors' house in our car with blackened headlights so as to give no hint of my arrival. After pulling up a hundred feet from their house, I groped my way around the trees and bushes in the darkness and approached the dimly lit porch, waiting for the sound of jingle bells that would be my signal to enter. During those several minutes in the cold winter air, I was struck by the realization that even though I didn't have a clue as to how to act once I got inside, I was more excited than anxious.

When I heard the bells I found myself moving across the porch and into the hall without willing it, as if propelled by an invisible hand, calling out, "HO, HO, HO, MERRRRRY CHRISTMAS!" surprised by the deep sound of my own voice. I entered a dreamland room, lit only by candlelight, filled with smiling, handsomely dressed people, the whole scene glowing with the soft, hazy quality of a Monet painting. As I moved across the floor with my bag of toys, the adults clapped and cheered, and several women kissed me, which I accepted as my due. I had never felt so welcomed or appreciated in my life.

Overwhelmed by my reception, it took me a moment to remember that I needed to turn my attention to the two children who were my reason for being there. The two-year-old girl was clearly not ready for the red and white apparition I had become, and she shrunk back in her mother's arms as I delivered her presents and spoke to her as soothingly as I could.

The five-year-old boy, Woody, was another matter altogether. This cute little man with his bowtie was not in the least intimidated and from the moment I looked at him, I could see that his eyes were locked on me with rapturous wonder. As I moved toward him, I became transfixed as well, so that everyone in the room fell away except for him and me. When I kneeled in front of him, listening to his Christmas wishes, every sound of his voice, every expression of his face, exuded trust and love. No one had *ever* looked at me like that. He was looking into the face of *God* – and so was I.

When I had heard him out and given him his presents, we hugged each other for a long moment, and then I was leaving to the sound of more cheering and clapping, not wanting to do anything but savor what had just happened. Not since my encounter with the doll-like dark haired girl at spin-the-bottle thirty years earlier had I been so instantly transformed, so thrilled to the very marrow of my being.

I can't say how convincing I was as Santa that night, and I don't know how much the reaction of those cheering, clapping people was motivated by kindness as opposed to my Santa charisma. What I do know is that for two people in that room, Woody and me, I wasn't a Santa, I was *the* Santa.

And I had to be forced to do it. I couldn't picture it. I didn't plan it, my brain fought it every inch of the way. But in the event, it didn't even require effort, instead I just gave in to it. More than any other experience of my life, playing Santa convinced me that I didn't know what I was doing here. It left me feeling that all I could do was to throw myself (or have Pat throw me) out into the traffic of life and be run over by unbidden experience.

For much of my life I have carried around a template of myself that I strove mightily to defend and protect, an image of someone who was in control, ahead of events, who mustn't look foolish. To protect that template, I established a kind of floating fortress around me to forestall being put in any situation that would tarnish that image. Whenever I was around other people, I had to look at least competent, or better yet, the master of events. This requires constant evaluation – Am I looking good or not? – and an enormous amount of effort trying to figure out what's going to happen next and cover all the bases.

That meant that when I first tried dancing in the eighth grade, I had projected what I ought to look like so much that my focus was on getting the mechanical action of the dance steps just right. As a result, I couldn't tune in to the beat of the music because my brain was working overtime willing my body to look a certain way. If you can't feel the beat, you can't dance.

So, I gave up and for the next twenty years of high school dances, fraternity parties, weddings and social occasions of every kind dreaded the prospect of being expected to dance. It was the Spanish Inquisition of my early life. After that extended stay on the torture rack, I was pretty stretched out of shape by the time Pat got ahold of me, and it took a while to peel back all those layers of tension. An odd thing is that she never showed any frustration or discouragement even though I acted pretty badly on occasion when she would force the issue of dancing.

An even odder thing is that when I finally did hear the beat, I discovered that dancing was not only easy, it was effortless, just as being Santa was effortless. The very process of calculating how to do it kept me from doing it. But when playing Santa, I couldn't for the life of me figure out what the steps were – I couldn't paint footprints on the floor the way they do in dance instruction books. There was no choreography that I could fixate on so I had to wing it, and when I did I stepped into a different world.

It has occurred to me that having Pat appear in my life was something like Dorothy landing in Oz – everything went from black and white to color. Black-and-white Kansas was all or nothing, a place of narrow limitations and impotence. Oz was a place of experimentation and discovery, where Dorothy and her friends had to break out of their constricted visions of themselves and realize the life – and the power – they had all along.

Computer scientists have a word for black-and-white Kansas, and for them it's a good thing. "Primitive" is a term of art in computer science that describes the unambiguous building blocks that make up algorithms. In so many ways, "primitive" describes my mentality for much of my life, always looking for those precisely located footsteps on the dance floor.

CHAPTER TWENTY-TWO

It's amazing how many lessons you can forget at the top of
your backswing.

Golf saying

Shortly after we bought our farm, I decided that I would satisfy one of my childhood fantasies: to become an airplane pilot. We had enough room for an airstrip on the property, and could base our plane within a hundred yards of the house. My plan was to eventually cover the seven-hundred-mile commute to the boatyard in Maine in my own plane, thus avoiding all the delays and hassles of airline travel. In the event, Pat decided to get her license as well (she actually got hers first) whereupon we bought a small single-engine plane to gain some flying time and built our airstrip.

That year (1985), when the time came to go to Maine for the summer, we decided that we would make our first flight there – an ambitious effort since neither of us had yet logged five hours of flying time since getting our licenses. The carefully drawn flight plan called for us to cross the Chesapeake Bay and then generally follow the coast to Maine, stopping in Connecticut to get fuel. Because our training, and therefore our licenses, limited us to VFR conditions (must be able to see the ground), we had to pick our weather carefully. On the appointed day, everything looked favorable.

I had hardly gotten the plane to cruising altitude over the Bay when I realized how hazy it was over the water on that warm, humid June day. Almost immediately, the horizon disappeared as the distant sky merged with the water and I was flying in IFR conditions (can't see the ground). As my pulse quickened, I focused on maintaining my planned altitude of five thousand feet and locked my vision on the altimeter with laser-like intensity. The altimeter looks like a clock, with the small hand indicating thousands of feet of altitude and the large hand indicating hundreds of feet. If those hands are rotating in a clockwise direction you are going up and, if counterclockwise, you're headed down.

As I stared at those hands, trying to will them to lock in place at five thousand feet, I discovered something very distressing. When I pushed or pulled on the control yoke (which controls altitude, at least in the short-term), there was a delay in the response of the altimeter to my inputs, so that I was overcorrecting for each off-altitude indication, constantly going through five thousand feet, but never staying there. The result was that the plane began to porpoise in an increasingly alarming fashion, giving us a not so fun rollercoaster ride. Pat said nothing through all this, either diplomatic, or frightened into silence, or both.

Just before losing control of the airplane, it occurred to me to try something different. I looked at the attitude indicator, which is a round gauge with a horizontal line drawn across the center of it with simulated airplane wings superimposed on the line when the plane is in a level attitude. If the wings are below the line, the plane is in a descending attitude, and vice versa. Unlike the altimeter, it responds immediately to changes in the plane's position. I realized I could hold the wings on the artificial horizon fairly easily, whereupon the plane leveled out and pulse rates dropped all around.

The trap I had fallen into, which has killed many thousands of pilots and passengers, is called "fixation," and avoiding it is drilled into every flying student – in my case, obviously not well enough. The idea is that when flying on instruments, the pilot does not fixate on one indicator, but maintains a "scan" of all the relevant gauges, using the information provided by each in an appropriate way. Scanning is a part of a larger principle of flying called "situational awareness," which can be loosely translated as "What's the most important thing right now, and what should I be doing about it?"

I couldn't do that, and the reason was that my mind was racing *ahead.* In those threatening moments, my thoughts jumped to the awful consequences to come – the rending crash of the plane into the water, the last terrible choking moments of drowning, the soggy corpses being wheeled into ambulances under the glare of TV camera lights, the sympathetic but patronizing assessment of friends and family that I had foolishly killed myself and my wife and made my children orphans in the process. In that crisis, my brain was so overwhelmed by speculation that it couldn't run its good pilot program but instead "locked up," in computer- speak, on a primitive number – five thousand, to be exact.

My brain has an incredible ability to store and process information – in this case, all that flying instruction. But, much more than manmade computers (an autopilot would have handled this situation just fine), it's prone to being distracted from its present job. In computer-speak, our brains are "noisy." So, whether it's avoiding fiery death or dealing with more mundane situations such managing diet, exercise or homework, it has trouble answering the question, "What is the most important thing right now and what should I be doing about it?"

CHAPTER TWENTY-THREE

A physicist is a Kantian fisherman who thinks
there are no fish smaller than the size of the mesh of his net.

John Ziman, British physicist

The idea that there is more to us than our physical being goes back a long way, the first evidence of which may be the burial rites of primitive humans some fifty thousand years ago, who buried their deceased family members with "grave gear" – tools, weapons, flowers – presumably representing the desire to help the deceased even though the old physical body was gone. Over time the descriptions of that unseen reality became more sophisticated in the form of supernatural stories that offered a connection to an omnipotent force that could break the seeming inevitability of the cause-and-effect cycle of life and death, providing purpose and hope.

So far, so good. Seen as a way for prescientific people to relate to the value of human life, these stories had value as supposedly factual accounts of events. But, like many educated people in the modern world, I couldn't believe those stories. The knowledge of both recorded history and science stored in my brain had produced a gatekeeper that wouldn't let them pass unchallenged.

At the same time, I knew that many educated people allowed their gatekeeper brains to simply slam the door on nonphysical reality by denying any kind of spontaneity, including free will, content with the notion that finite cause-and-effect was the only force at work in the world. In such a world *nothing* matters because it's going to happen *anyway*. For me, such a notion is the ultimate default to the limitations of the brain and more fantastic than the most bizarre primitive creation mythology.

Thus, I had been incapable of accepting this logical conundrum of futility in the same way that I had been unable to buy into traditional religions, however comforting they might be. In both cases, my gatekeeper brain had prevented me from seeing an acceptable view of what my life is about.

Yet by seeing my brain as a dedicated mechanical device with limited capabilities, I could see that everything didn't have to be run through its filter, that the gatekeeper shouldn't guard the whole house but only the mechanical equipment, that it knew nothing about the living spaces. In order for that idea to make sense, I had to get clear about the notion that there was a lot that my brain not only didn't get, but was not capable of getting.

This was something I had been thinking about since childhood, but only in a casual way. I remember in my ninth-grade science class learning about what was then known about the size of the universe and wondering how it could be limited. I would actually try to visualize chunks of space, one after another, each going beyond the last until a stopping place, but I couldn't do it. There was always that space beyond. When I forced myself to try to finish this train of thought, my head actually began to hurt, as if I was tying my brain into a knot. Since as a fourteen-year-old I had more immediate concerns than infinity, I didn't torture myself too much with this problem, but I filed it away somewhere to have it come up repeatedly over the years whenever I would think about cosmic subjects.

More recently, it has occurred to me with respect to the Big Bang Theory of the beginning of the universe, which postulates that the visible universe is the aftermath of an explosion that occurred billions of years ago. When I hear that I automatically ask the question, "Okay, so where did the explosive material come from?" I don't mean to say that all this research isn't worth doing, only that, in this context, the word "beginning" must be a reference to an intermediate rather than ultimate event. How can our world be the "effect" of a "cause"?

I know that one possible answer is that science has solved so many riddles in the last few hundred years that it's only a matter of time before the problem of understanding infinity can be conquered – the relentless march of science carried to its extreme. But that answer contradicts itself because all scientific discoveries, including the most cosmic, are dependent on the limits of finite measurement. This limitation is aptly captured by the saying among scientists (particularly mathematicians) that "God is a mathematician."

When Einstein formulated his special theory of relativity in 1905, he also postulated the formula for which he is best known, $E = mc^2$. That formula describes a fixed relationship, which was not fully accepted in the scientific world until it could be verified by experiments that confirmed it. Similarly, his general theory of relativity, introduced in 1916, said not only that gravity bends light, but also by exactly how much, and Einstein was not given full credit for this discovery until it was confirmed by astronomers in 1919 with precise measurement.

When Werner Heisenberg formulated his uncertainty principle in 1927, it led to an identity crisis among physicists because he said that not only is there something we don't know about the behavior of subatomic particles, but there is something we *can't know*. We cannot simultaneously measure a subatomic particle's momentum and position. This might not sound earthshaking to laymen, but to physicists it was like running into a brick wall. The whole thrust of their profession is to postulate and then verify a fixed, predictable framework for physical phenomena, and here was a dead end. The uncertainty principle was so much of a dead end that Einstein couldn't accept it and thereby alienated himself from mainstream physics, which grudgingly accepted Heisenberg's principle, for the rest of his life.

Science's answer to this dead end was to do what science must always do – put a number on it. They did this by calculating the statistical probability of a large number of particles behaving in a measurable way and then verifying *that* measurement.

At some remove, what we can know about cause and effect must break down, just as infinite largeness or smallness defies measurement – they're both *endless*.

The human brain has about *1,000,000,000,000,000* synapses. That's a lot. But how can it even cross the starting line when it comes to figuring out how all this got started or where it's going and, more importantly, what signifies for us as human beings?

Anyone who has had children is familiar with the characteristic of toddlers who engage in the frustrating habit of saying "why" to successive answers to their questions.

Child: "Why do birds sing?"

Mom: "Because they're happy."

Child: "Why?"

Mom: "Because the sun is shining."

Child: "Why?"

Mom: "Because it makes them feel good."

Child: "Why?"

Mom: "Because it just does."

The child is just waking up to the processes of the adult rational world in which there seems to be a cause-and-effect explanation for everything. If you brush your teeth you won't get cavities. Looking both ways before crossing the street means not getting hit by a car. If you eat all your dinner you'll get dessert. It seems that one thing always leads to another – all cause and effect. So, what the questioning child is doing is just taking the "why?" business to its logical conclusion. The problem for the inquisitive child and the frustrated mom is that there is no ultimate logical conclusion. Behind every "because" there's always another "why?".

Why, after all, do birds sing? Because it's an evolutionary trait calculated to attract mates and make for more birds? Would a trillion birds be better than a billion birds? Why have birds at all?

CHAPTER TWENTY-FOUR

A thing of beauty is a joy forever.

John Keats

Hinckley's survival following the luxury tax crisis gave all of us in the company a chance to exhale. But after that exhalation, I had to come to grips with the fact that our long-term prospects were not good. While the powerboat market was thriving, interest in sailboats in general and cruising sailboats in particular was declining. Sailboats may be the slowest form of transportation, requiring considerable patience and skill to operate, and the cultural trend, then as now, was towards speed and user friendliness.

I had bought the Hinckley Company because I wanted to get beyond where I was in the hotel business – focused on the financial endgame, enduring for the present. Instead, I wanted the present experience of creating and sharing beauty. But, to have that opportunity, I had to reckon with the fact that the Hinckley Company was just like the hotel business in this way: you have to have enough customers to cover the costs of running the business. And, while that long-term cultural trend wasn't the brick wall of the luxury tax, it was almost worse. Congress wasn't going to fix it, and I could only too well picture that lingering death – the waterlogged barge of fixed expenses being slowly sucked down into the whirlpool of a declining customer base. For several years, I struggled with this seemingly unavoidable prospect, frustrated and depressed.

Finally, I hit bottom, and decided that if we were building something customers were no longer excited about, we would build something that *I* was excited about – and it would not be a sailboat, but a powerboat. The source of that excitement came from my childhood, when, in a singular act of generosity, my father gave me a thirteen-foot Lyman wooden runabout with a ten-horsepower Johnson outboard motor. With its varnished mahogany, copper fitted interior, and white lapstrake hull, it remains one of the most beautiful boats I have ever seen. Requiring less than a foot of water in which to operate, a buddy and I would use it to explore shallow creeks and uninhabited islands, cooking small fish over a campfire, sleeping under the stars – we were the Lewis and Clark of mid-fifties Chesapeake, Virginia.

Could we recreate that restraint-free, adventurous opportunity for grown-up Hinckley customers? I thought we could, and I could see the template for that boat out of the window of my apartment on the Hinckley dock every day I was there. It was not a recreational boat, but a commercial one – the traditional Maine lobster boat. With their upswept bow, low profile, and small pilothouse, these boats seemed to skim over the water while their less graceful brethren plowed through it.

To make that template a yacht, I went to three successive naval architects. I will never forget the moment I opened the mailing tube from the last of them, Bruce King, and saw the preliminary drawing of what was to become the Hinckley Picnic Boat. It was stunningly beautiful, even on paper, and I immediately reached for the telephone to call Bruce to lock it in, afraid that this apparition of the boat of my dreams would vanish before my eyes.

Even as I instantly fell in love with what this boat could be, I understood it might not be an easy sell, either within or outside the company. For a thirty-six-foot boat, the sleeping, cooking, and even cabin headroom was minimal, and when built to Hinckley's customary standards of quality and finish, it would be absurdly expensive for its size.

In the event, I didn't sell it within the company. My partner, Bob, gave me the benefit of the doubt, and everyone else just went along with the boss, incredulous. I later learned that when Bruce King came to the company for a visit, our company general manager pulled him aside and said, "Can you get him off this thing and onto something that will make us some money?" For my part, I was too excited to do anything but charge ahead.

As for the shallow water capability that made my Lyman such a magic carpet for exploration and adventure, I had an idea about that. Conventional boats have some form of propeller and rudder that hang below the hull to provide thrust and control. But there was an alternative, little used on larger boats because it is less efficient and more expensive: a water jet. In the simplest terms, it is a powerful firehose pointed behind the boat that pushes it along, just as a jet engine pushes an airplane along. Despite its expense and diminished efficiency, the jet has a number of advantages. Because nothing hangs below the hull, a jet-powered boat can safely run in very shallow water, allowing it to be used in many places that a conventional boat cannot go. And because steering and reversing is accomplished by rotating that firehose nozzle, thrust is smoothly and infinitely variable. There is nothing quite like it.

Yet when we located and tested one of the rare existing large boats that had a jet, I could see that while there was wonderful control authority, harnessing that authority would be difficult, not least because the jet has opposite sensing in reverse from a conventional boat, or, for that matter, a car. What it cried out for was a computerized fly-by-wire joystick control system that would take full advantage of that smoothness and variability, creating an intuitive relationship between boater and boat. Because nothing like it existed at the time, I decided we would have to do it ourselves.

Since no one at Hinckley seemed to have any enthusiasm for the joystick, I opted to develop it near my home in Maryland where I spent most of my time. To get it done I went to a young man named Kent Fadeley, who had no formal training as an engineer yet was a true polymath, which is to say someone who can learn to do anything, though only things that fascinate him. Oblivious to money, he could not be hired, but he could be enticed. I enticed him. With Kent's help, we hired a computer hardware and software engineer who worked out of his garage, and the three of us set off to create an electronic joystick control system. Over the following year, we went through a lot of joysticks, circuit boards, software, and near disasters, but in the end we did it. It was to become the first joystick in the recreational boating industry, a technology that has only now become broadly accepted.

Back at Hinckley we had set up a shop dedicated to building the first Picnic Boat, and there was plenty of curiosity about the project, not only in the company but in the larger hotbed of boatbuilding that is that part of Maine. So, when the day came in June of 1994 to launch it there was a large crowd of professional critics on hand to watch. When I had gotten clear of the dock, I pushed the throttle forward and it leaped up on the surface like a big surfboard, seeming to barely touch the surface. When I tried a sharp turn, it instantly swapped ends, a maneuver we subsequently dubbed the "bat turn." When the time came to return, I was able, with the joystick, to move the boat sideways into the dock, something like moving a car sideways into a parallel parking space. Handling it was totally different from a conventional boat and utterly fun – a kind of floating amusement park. And, as I embarked on demonstrating it to others, including prospective customers, everyone agreed that it was pretty and enjoyed their turn.

Yet, despite that appreciation, the most essential attribute of a successful boat – sales – had not shown itself. Over the course of that summer, I must have taken out dozens of prospects, with not so much as a nibble.

In terms of a new boat introduction, that wasn't just disappointing, it was disastrous. When I walked around the boatyard that summer, increasingly, people I knew well avoided eye contact with me, and as the end of August – and the selling season – approached, the Picnic Boat was looking like a commercial failure, a black eye for the Hinckley Company in general and for me in particular.

The last week of August I was down at the Hinckley dock sitting on the Picnic Boat, kind of like a kid with a lemonade stand on the side of the road. A man I had never met walked up and asked for a ride. As I took the boat through my now standard maneuvers, he said little. When we returned, he stepped onto the dock, leaving me with that familiar sinking feeling. Then he turned to face me, held out his right hand to shake mine, held up two fingers with his left hand, and said, "Congratulations, I'll take two." It turned out he was a wealthy South American yachtsman who planned to keep one of the boats in Maine and the other at his home in Argentina.

That opened the floodgates. By the end of the year, we had sold seven Picnic Boats, and the following year we sold twenty. In a short time, the Hinckley Company was transformed from a small sailboat company to a much larger jet boat company. In 2016, the one thousandth Hinckley jet boat was delivered.

What happened? When the sailboat market began to evaporate, I was trapped in my brain's programmed envelope of what we could do as a company and what customers would want, leaving me wallowing in self-pity and impotence. Only when I was able to look back into my own personal childhood experience could I get in touch with *what makes boating worth doing at all* – excitement – and begin to share it with others. Then, I was caught by something so attractive I couldn't and didn't want to resist it, heedless of all the rational reasons why I shouldn't do it. It would be hard to make it a business school case study, hard to understand in terms of strategic "critical thinking." Of course, I was not oblivious to profit margins and recovery of capital, but my part in the thing was not strategic planning, nor was it hands-on – I am a hopeless mechanic. My essential contribution was excitement, a passion for which there is no "why."

CHAPTER TWENTY-FIVE

It is because we don't know who we are, because we are
unaware that the Kingdom of Heaven is within us, that we
behave in the generally silly, the often insane, the sometimes
criminal ways that are so characteristically human.

Aldous Huxley

But if my brain can't get what really matters, how do *I* get it? In
other words, if *I* am not my brain, what and where is my *self* that
does get it?

I sure know what and where my brain is. It's a glob of grey stuff in
my head with specific physical dimensions and characteristics and, even
though I don't much like the thought of it, it can be taken out of my head
and put in a jar on the shelf as in old horror movies. My *self,* however,
cannot be quantified or located, nor do I even have any words to define
it. So, for the scientifically-minded, it's hard to explain what the *self* is.

And in our world, it's hard not to be scientifically-minded. Unlike early
humans, who had to deal with an environment that was unexplainable,
we have concrete explanations for almost everything about our physical
environment, and we can believe in and depend on them. Right now,
I know that when I hit "a" on the keyboard of my laptop, "a" is going
to appear on the screen and will do it every time. Every time I turn

the thermostat up, the temperature in the house is going to the level I set, no higher and no lower. Our whole technological world, including communication, transportation, medicine, clothing, and food, has, as its foundation, dependable, measurable, hard-edged science.

Not only is science credible, but the most persistent, organized attempt to connect with the *self* (read soul) in the industrialized West is religion, which we inherited from those early humans who were ignorant of science, and which is incredible because it relies on miraculous stories most of us don't believe ever happened.

How, then, to accept and appreciate the existence of the *self?* The answer, I believe, is to recognize the difference between being scientifically-*minded* and scientifically-*limited*. Science has brought us a level of safety and comfort that would have been unthinkable for those early humans and is an integral part of modern life. But its very nature is to speak in terms of limitation, narrowly distinguishing one object, phenomenon, or result from another, which is to say that it can't address the most important things, which defy boundaries and limits. How do you distinguish one love from another or one beauty from another? Sure, you can engage in an intellectual exercise of doing so, pushing them out at arm's length, but to what end?

We don't need to know what *God* looks like, how tall He is, what He weighs, or where, geographically, He lives. We just need to know that He is the unlimited personification of all that is good and right. And the same thing can be said about the *self*. While my body may be different from yours, my brain may have different abilities and programming than yours, my *self* is the personification of all that is good and right, just as yours is. We simply paint on different canvases.

And how can I know that? Let me start by asking, "How do we know anything?" It's a subject philosophers have struggled with for thousands of years, and they have a fancy word for it – epistemology. In the scientifically-minded modern world, we tend to think of knowledge as finite conclusions that can be stored in and retrieved from our brains.

Yet there is another kind of knowing that is not transmitted from the outside but arises spontaneously within us, and is so obvious that in the maze of everyday activities we tend to see right past it. It is not a finite conclusion, but a knowing that comes from asking, "Am I the person I am capable of being right now?" The difficulty with recognizing the *self* that asks this question is that it is constantly being suppressed by our computational brains.

And how do *I* know that? *I* know that because that's been my *experience*. *I* knew that it would feel good to share my childhood epiphanies, but *if this, then that* would mean I would be ridiculed. *I* knew it would be good to show some empathy and love to Barbara during her psychological meltdown, but *if this, then that* would make it that much harder to abandon a relationship that I secretly wanted to get out of. *I* knew that I felt lousy about concealing my desire to leave the law firm from those I had encouraged and supported until the last minute, rather than being honest about my evolving desires, but, *if this, then that* would lead to messy discussions that I didn't have the courage to face.

The *self* that knows these things is sometimes called the "still, small voice" that lies within us, and has all too easily been shouted down by my mechanical brain putting up impenetrable walls of cause and effect. Yet this self is more valuable *and real* than any knowledge that can be defined.

CHAPTER TWENTY-SIX

Happiness is the only good
The time to be happy is now
The place to be happy is here
The way to be happy
Is to make others so

Robert Ingersol

When I held my first grandchild in my arms five minutes after his birth, I was overwhelmed with the sense that this helpless infant was going to be my teacher. And so it was. In the ensuing months and years, I was often Kyle's caregiver – babysitting, feeding, and dressing him – but those mechanical functions were just to allow me to be with him so that I could see the world anew through his eyes. That world was fresh, exciting, and always changing. We had an unspoken pact that we would dig into the very marrow of what was in front of us – an ice cycle became a magic wand, a mud puddle a funhouse. When he would fall asleep on my lap I felt not just trusted, but honored. And when he was cranky and demanding, it was easy to remember how often I was that way myself and laugh at all that silly drama. I was him and he was me.

What Kyle and I had to offer each other was who we were inside. Before, when I felt such passion, I wanted something. Even with Pat, I wanted to possess her, physically and emotionally, and I was busy calculating potential threats that might mean losing her. I was also constantly judging her to see if she measured up to my expectations. For all the joy she brought me, in my brain she was still a prisoner of my fears and desires. But with Kyle I wasn't afraid or judging, because everything about him was unexpected and unjudgable. This want of calculation left me not just loving Kyle, but loving myself.

This was a new experience, and allowed a profound realization. For most of my life, I not only hadn't loved myself, I hadn't even *liked* me. How can you like someone who pretends to be someone they're not, who makes secret calculations to manipulate other people, and who is so distracted and afraid that they can't empathize with their fellow human beings? It was as if I was dirty.

But with Kyle, I was washed clean, and I was loveable.

The summer that Kyle turned four, I took my annual trip to Quebec to fish for salmon. At this point I had not missed many chances to spend time with him – he lived just across the yard. This separation between us of ten days was to be the longest since he had been old enough to be aware of such things, and Pat and I had gone to some pains to explain to him that Grandpa was going away but would be back soon. The day of my departure we had a family gathering at the farm and, for most of the afternoon, Kyle and I were even more glued together than usual. When the time came for me to get in my car, neither Kyle nor I wanted our hug to end, and I drove off, wondering if any salmon fishing could be as good as what I was leaving. Later I learned that he had run after the car as I drove out of the driveway.

About five days into the trip, I drove from the salmon camp into town to call home and check on everyone. When I got through to Pat, we talked for about ten minutes, and then she said there was someone there who wanted to talk to me. When she handed the phone to Kyle, I tried to get him to talk, but all I could hear on the other end of the line was the sound of his breathing, and I began to despair of him saying anything. Finally, after a long pause in my coaxing, he said two words, softly but firmly, more command than plea: "Come home."

At the end of the trip, when I had gotten in my car after landing in Washington, I called Pat, who said she would get Kyle so he would be there when I got home. When, at last, I pulled up to the front of our house, I got out of the car and walked toward the door. I could see Kyle on the other side of the screen door, playing in the entrance hall. As I approached the steps, he turned to look at me, smiled, raised his fingertips up under his chin as if in prayer, and then began clapping in slow motion. As we both walked up to the door, he put his index finger against the screen and I put mine opposite his, and for most of a minute we traced designs together, the skin of our fingertips separated only by the thin mesh of wire.

Neither of us had yet uttered a sound.

CHAPTER TWENTY-SEVEN

There are two kinds of people in the world:
Those who divide the world into two parts,
And those who don't.

Robert Benchley

The first philosophy course I took in college was Logic 201, and I have never forgotten the lesson on the first day: "The whole world is either A or Non-A – e.g., the whole world is either this chair I'm sitting in or it's not this chair I'm sitting in. Nothing exists but this chair and everything that is not this chair." I didn't know whether the statement was absurd or brilliant – at once useless and undeniable. Was it a glib and meaningless linguistic stunt, or was it an incisive surgical stroke pointing the way to how to organize and understand every constituent part of world?

That lesson in Logic 201 haunted me for years until I began to get some sense of what that was about for me. Separating the world into A and Non-A was the right analogy for my default to the notion that hard-edged logic was the lens through which I should view the whole world.

Wasn't that what I had been trying to do since I settled on my plan for success as an alienated child? Either I would be a respected achiever or I wouldn't; either I would look like a real man (loyal, with a manageable wife who would make me look good) or I wouldn't; either I would be a financial success or I wouldn't – not just no middle ground, but an end that was not just defined (A), but that excluded any other possibility (Non-A). What happened in the meantime was just to be gotten through until I could arrive at that concrete, crucial result.

And because the goal was so clearly and unforgivingly defined and excluded everything else, it was a life-or-death proposition and each intermediate step leading to it became a life-or-death proposition as well. As I completed my swing on one trapeze, there had to be another there in precisely the right place to grab or I was in freefall. How could I even think about anything else, much less be happy, when there was a *possibility* that I would fail the bar exam?

For most of my life there had seemed to be a lot of trapezes out in front of me, and I could cherish the vague notion that, at the end of the line, the last one would catapult me into heaven – to a place where I didn't have to be desperately grasping for the next thing. All the pieces would be in place. And then, when all those pieces were in place, everything I planned for and fantasized about had come to pass. I did pass the bar exam, I was a successful lawyer, I did get money, position, and a wonderful wife. And yet much of the time, I was still out there doing my aerial trapeze act, behaving as if the next accomplishment or event, however trivial, was all or nothing, life or death.

There is a corridor in our house between the family room and our bedroom where we set up cribs for our grandchildren. That worked quite well while they were infants, but when the oldest became four they needed more sleeping room than a crib can provide. Pat's solution to this problem was to put full-size bunkbeds in this fairly narrow (seven-foot) space, which is our only access to our bedroom. I agreed to this only reluctantly because it seemed to me to leave too small a space for comfortable passage.

Unfortunately, the bunk bed arrived and was being set up just as we were beginning a birthday dinner for our daughter-in-law. To my disgust I saw that not only was the bed itself wider than I had feared, but it required an angled ladder to reach the top bunk, which further narrowed the passage to the bedroom. When I complained about this, Pat made a remark that seemed to me to make light of my concern.

It was a spark falling on dry tinder.

I rounded on her like a cornered wolf, letting her know in no uncertain terms that the goddamned thing was not going to stay there and initiating an exchange of words that couldn't have been any fun for my daughter-in-law, son and grandchildren to hear or see. The dinner proceeded from then on in a somber note, more resembling a wake than a birthday party.

The problem wasn't that there couldn't be a legitimate discussion between my wife and me regarding the arrangement of our shared living space. The bunk bed was fine, we just moved the ladder out of the way when the kids weren't using it. Rather, it was that a totally unwanted response was triggered in my brain that saw the issue as all or nothing, a life-or-death question that had to be settled *right then*. I had done something destructive and useless that spoiled an otherwise happy occasion – the last thing I wanted to do – and the craziest part was that I *knew* I was doing it but couldn't stop myself.

Afterwards I realized that in that moment of confrontation with Pat, I saw it as *all or nothing* – a crucial test of whether I was going to be the master in my own house or not, whether Pat was going to emasculate me totally or not, whether I was going to revert to being a powerless child with no control over my destiny or not.

Historically, this mechanical separation of life into two opposing categories is found in the philosophical concept of the "pair of opposites." The notion is that there is the eternal spiritual place were all is united and one, and then there is the earthly realm of time and space where everything is based on opposites – good and evil, right and wrong, male and female, birth and death, A and Non-A. In this context, heaven transcends opposites, so that the lion lays down with the lamb, since there is no predator-prey relationship and all is at peace. When I studied Buddhism and Hinduism I learned that this has been one of the most persistent concepts in philosophical thought going all the way back to original Sanskrit texts, and that the ancient world is filled with graphic representations of this idea.

Christian mythology reflects this in the story of the garden of Eden where female is created as an opposite to male and the act of eating from the tree of good and evil drives humanity out of the heavenly paradise into the world of temporal struggle. What I learned in church as a child was that this was all about the evil snake, the faithless Eve, and Adam's lack of backbone, and that all of us owed God for this incredible screw-up by the first humans. All in all, not a pretty picture, but read in terms of traditional mythology, the story is simply about human beings coming into the realm of earthly existence where there is a tension between yin and yang, all is not peace, and there are plenty of problems.

My sense is that the whole reason for talking about the pairs of opposites is to address how we allow ourselves to be constantly pulled in opposite directions. Down in the trenches it's hard to see the horizon and easy to get confused by the panoply of comparisons, judgments and choices.

There's so much to think about! After all, there are many possibilities for the future, and most of the potential outcomes are not what we want. I sure want to keep what I've got, but I also want other things that I think will make my life better. By "things" I mean some scenario, whether it's having possessions, relationships, status or a particular environment. All of these things are finite and identifiable, at least in my imagination, and I expect that if I can do the right engineering, I'll keep what I have and get what I want. It's a rolling process of reducing A to a "primitive" and then separating it out from Non-A – everything else.

Thinking in this way helped me to see what those sages always understood: the world of time and space that our brains see is about finite mechanical separation – hard-edged, measurable and unforgiving – and that the "eternal" place is where mechanics and comparison are left behind and everything blends together.

CHAPTER TWENTY-EIGHT

As the light grows, we see ourselves as worse
than we thought. We are amazed at our former
blindness as we see issuing from our heart
A whole swarm of shameful feelings, like filthy
reptiles crawling from a hidden cave. But we
must be neither amazed or disturbed.
We are not worse than we were:
On the contrary, we are better.

Francis de Sales

One of the parts of Christianity that I didn't understand when I was growing up was the need for forgiveness. It wasn't that I didn't know I'd done things I wished I hadn't or that I continued to think and act in ways that were harmful to me and others, but that focusing on a release in the future was a distraction from doing better in the present.

Now I want to think that no matter what my failings have been in the past, every new day is an opportunity to be a great human being. To do that, I need to immediately and directly confront the source of those failings – my brain – and catch it before it gets up to its old tricks. One way of doing this is to enter into literal debates with it in the moment that exposes its craziness to the light of day. Some examples:

I stop at a convenience store and find myself at the end of a long checkout line.

Brain: What a pain! This is going to take forever.

Me: It doesn't matter. It's not like I have some important thing to do when I get home.

Brain: But look at these people – you know your time is more important than theirs. Besides, that guy with the tattoos who's taking so long is buying cigarettes and lottery tickets. How stupid!

Me: It's not as if I don't know, respect and admire people who are tattooed, smoke, and/or buy lottery tickets. Is this arrogance making me feel better?

After this response, my anger quickly melts away and, almost as quickly, the line melts away, and I am on my way, feeling better about myself than I did when I entered the store.

Another: I sit down to work on this book right after I wake up in the morning.

Brain: You're feeling pretty groggy this morning. You can work on the book later.

Me: You just don't want to focus. You're stalling.

Brain: Look around this room. You've been telling yourself you want to hang the pictures you've had sitting on the floor forever and throw out a lot of stuff in here that you'll never use again. This place is a mess and you need to get it cleaned.

Me: You're stalling.

Brain: Let's get something straight! I'm in charge here. Remember when you were in college and you promised yourself you'd get term papers out of the way sooner rather than later? What happened then?

Me: You kept finding ways to distract me so that they were written at the last minute and poor.

Brain: Yeah, and that's how it is now. You've been working on this thing for fifteen years and still aren't finished. Besides, even if you do finish it, no one's going to read it.

Me: Do you even like me?

Brain: You've got a lot of other things to think about! What about that dark spot on your back? It could be a melanoma. Those things spread fast and you could be dead in six months. What would the memorial service be like? Peter Egeli (a close friend) would probably give one of the eulogies and say some great things about you.

Me: I'm going to let you exhaust yourself with this madness, and then I'm going to write.

After a short while, my brain does exhaust itself, and I am able to write several paragraphs, leaving me feeling good about this small victory and reminding me why I'm writing this book.

And another:

Pat is constantly arranging occasions at our house to host events for members of our family and extended family. Often this can include thirty people or more, yet her talent and energy never flags. For my part, I sometimes feel that I'm living on an anthill.

Brain: Well, here you are again. Look at how much effort she's putting into preparing food for all these people. She sure doesn't do that for you. And she knows you don't have much tolerance for crowds and does this anyway.

Me: All true, but it is a joy to watch someone who can create such a happy space for so many other people. Maybe I'm not the center of the universe.

Brain: You're not just some random person in the universe! You made the money that bought this place and that's paying for everything she's doing. She doesn't appreciate that and neither do all these people, who ought to be coming up to you, one by one, telling you how great you are, instead of thanking her for what she's doing.

Me: Maybe I should live here by myself and keep all my money.

Brain: That's not the point! This is a matter of simple justice. She owes you for the life you've made possible for her. Anyway, you're not all that desirable as a man and she wouldn't be here at all if you didn't have all that money.

Me: Yes, and if she wasn't beautiful, I wouldn't be here at all. Are you suggesting changing the way the world actually works?

At this point, it occurs to me that what is happening around me *is* actually the way the world works, and I might as well be a part of it, and start helping with the food preparation. As I do this, people begin talking to me and I start to relax. By the end of the day, I find that I have enjoyed myself.

My brain is constantly generating garbage, not to be picked up on Monday and Thursday mornings, but to be disposed of the moment it is produced. This is a constant 24/7 practice for which there is no substitute. My devil's workshop never closes.

CHAPTER TWENTY-NINE

We move ahead without the facts and learn them
as we go along.

Henry Ford

In the course of developing the joystick for Hinckley, I was referred to a man who was described to me as one "who knew more about boat motion control than anyone in the world" and who had pioneered motion control systems for fast passenger ferries, which, without those controls, were called "vomit comets." He had the very ordinary name of John Adams, but as we became acquainted I realized that he was anything but ordinary. He wasn't just an engineer, but a scientist of the best sort, at once creative and thorough. I had hoped to enlist his help in designing the joystick, but the owners of his company weren't interested. Still, he helped me informally and we became friends.

Several years later (2002), after I had sold Hinckley and John had left his company to become an industry consultant, he called to tell me he had something to show me. When I arrived, I saw a metal cube about thirty inches square sitting on the floor that contained a gyroscope designed to limit boat roll. It was made by a Japanese company, and he wanted to know what I thought of it. I was intrigued as he took the cover off and showed me the gyro flywheel, which, when spun at speed and allowed to tilt back and forth, would counteract roll motion. John explained that these "control moment gyroscopes" had been around for more than a hundred years but had never gained wide acceptance on boats, their principal use being to stabilize satellites in space. I was fascinated by the physics of the thing, which is a kind of gravity in a bottle, the only thing comparable I could think of being magnetism. How was it that I had never heard of this?

But I also saw the problem with its application, at least in the device I was looking at. It was too big, too heavy, and required too much power for the benefit it could provide. But as we talked, it became apparent to both of us that those problems could be solved by applying recently developed technologies. The first of those technologies was to spin the flywheel in a vacuum chamber to eliminate air friction, allowing it to spin faster – that's one of the reasons the things work so well in space. The second was to incorporate computerized motion sensors, like those used in the antilock brakes in your car, to regulate the tilting of the flywheel to match the wave energy.

As I drove home from my meeting with John, I couldn't stop thinking about the gyro. Nor could I stop thinking about it during the following sleepless night. There's a reason why "Don't rock the boat" is a common expression for upsetting things. What if that enduring problem could be solved in such a magical way? It wouldn't just benefit people who were already boating, but draw in many people who had been put off by the discomfort and seasickness of boat roll.

The next morning I went back to John's office and, as I later heard him describe it, "grabbed him by the collar, dragged him to the floor, and demanded that we start a gyro company." John, who was much better equipped than I to understand just how difficult it was going to be, must have been overwhelmed by my enthusiasm to the point that he abandoned sensible caution and agreed to do it.

As we embarked on setting up our new company, I set out to do it differently. By this time, I had been working on the ideas introduced in this book and wanted to put them to work in my life. I knew, despite high moments, how anxious I had been most of my business life and wanted to put myself in a position to avoid that. I also realized that I couldn't entirely stop my brain's relentless destructive expectation – outcome anxiety and all the perverse behavior that goes with it – but I could do some things to head it off.

So I would attempt to frame the venture in a way that said we're going to have fun with this as a present experience, independent of the ultimate outcome. As a child, I had enjoyed Donald Duck comic books, and particularly their offshoot comics, which featured Scrooge McDuck, Donald's rich uncle. Scrooge employed the services of an eccentric inventor named "Gyro Gearloose," who solved particularly difficult technical problems for Scrooge and had a muse always flitting around who had a lightbulb for a head. "Gearloose Engineering" would be our company name and the gyro muse would be our logo.

But I didn't want to frame just the company, I wanted to frame my part in it. As majority owner, it would have been conventional to give myself the title of CEO, which would have left me feeling that I had advertised myself as some kind of superior being who had all the answers. To get off that precarious pedestal from the start, the face of my business card would read, "Shepard Mckenney, CADQ*," and the back, "*Chief Asker of Dumb Questions."

CHAPTER THIRTY

Expectation is the source of all unhappiness.

Buddha

An archaic expression for a con artist is "projector," which is to say someone who persuades their victim to give up present value in return for an illusory future return – pyramid schemes, bogus stock offerings, and the like. My brain is a projector, always obsessing about how things are going to turn out, blinding me to what is happening right in front of me. But what if all my expectations were realized? Is a good life getting what you expected?

One clue is adjectives. When someone has had an unusually good experience, they are likely to say "wonderful," "fantastic," or "unbelievable" – all conveying a sense of transcending the predictable or even rational. Beside those words, "just what I wanted" is a consolation prize. Another is the way we go about doing something special for someone. A surprise party is better than just a party. A gift is better if the surprise isn't "ruined."

Perhaps the best example of the value of defying expectation is humor. I'm not talking about laughing at other people, but at myself. When I can laugh at how I've been staggering around in the dark, having my expectations frustrated at every turn, it doesn't just lift an oppressing weight, it's a happy teaching moment. Humor is about catching your brain going the wrong way, and the more I catch it doing that, the more I learn its limits. There have been few times in my life, no matter how seemingly disappointing or tragic at the time, that I could not have enjoyed a spiritual release by simply laughing at my foolish, self-defeating expectations.

Is there any way around the tyranny of expectation? The religion I grew up in seemed to promise that escape, just not in this life. Heaven was depicted as a place where everyone and everything was good all the time. Yet, when I allow myself to give up my narrow expectations, I don't go to a future heaven, *it comes to me – now.* But there's no predicting how or when that's going to happen.

Yes, heaven is a place where miracles happen, it's just that those miracles are not the first definition in the dictionary, "Contradicts known scientific laws," but the second, "Too good to be true." They are a surprise because they come out of nowhere.

When Kyle was ten months old he had a little plastic four-wheeled cart with an angled handle that looked something like a push lawn mower, designed for kids learning to walk. After he had learned to push this thing around standing up but before he had taken his first unaided step, he spent the night with Pat and me. For some reason, we all got up unreasonably early – before dawn, and this was late May – and the three of us were playing in the center hall of our house under the twinkling light of the brass chandelier. Pat was sitting on the floor at one end of the thirty-foot hall and I at the other, facing each other with our legs spread out in a V. Kyle would push his cart between us, ever faster, crashing into us at the end of each trip, laughing with excitement and enormously pleased with himself, but perhaps not as pleased or laughing as hard as were Pat and I.

We were in our own little universe of uncontrolled mirth.

After he had made a number of these commutes, he headed for me in the now usual fashion, when, at about ten feet from me and without warning, he shoved the cart aside, stretched his arms out toward me, and ran, collapsing against me with his arms tightly wrapped around my neck.

I think it took a few moments for each of us to take in what had happened. It reminded me of nothing so much as the classic scene in the faith healer's tent when the handicapped man from the audience throws down his crutches and walks confidently and gloriously, thanks to the ministrations of the preacher. The difference here was that Kyle had shared this physical manifestation of the discovery of his burgeoning life with me as a gift – a gift that he offered to Pat a few moments later.

That image of Kyle reaching toward me, taking the biggest risk of his young life, trusting me so much I could feel it in my body, reminds me that by its very nature, a miracle is a surprise.

And the same thing can be said of rituals.

Kyle had his sixth birthday party by the pool at our house. Our tradition is to make hand-cranked ice cream on summer birthdays as we did when my brothers and I were kids. So, after assistance by Kyle and a few of our young guests with ice, salt, some perfunctory cranking on their part and some hard cranking on mine, the ice cream is ready. As I stoop down to serve it out with birthday cake to a crowd of mostly unfamiliar six-year-old faces, it is a scene of bedlam, with kids running, squealing, and laughing, and the moms talking loudly to each other over the din about daycare, incompetent husbands, and the great party last week.

In the midst of all this I am content with the notion that Kyle is so totally stimulated that he has forgotten about me and my part in the thing. Suddenly he appears in front of me, and, for the next forty-five seconds, Kyle and I are in our own little bubble, the volume on all outside noise having been turned down. He looks into my eyes, and without saying a thing, quite deliberately takes a piece of cake from his plate with his spoon and puts it in my mouth and then does the same for himself. Next, he carefully repeats both gestures with the ice cream. Then my six-year-old priest is wordlessly gone, melted into the swirling mass of children.

Something has been unnecessarily lost in the overwhelming pervasiveness of science. While I know of no credible evidence that magic can be engineered, it exists in a realm beyond the brain. The computer and science exist in the world of calculation, prediction and verification. You make it happen, and then you must make it happen again – and if you can't, it's not real.

Magic can't be arranged, rather it happens unbidden. In fact, the process of trying to force it through my brain is the very thing that breaks the spell, just as trying to measure subatomic particles changes their behavior.

CHAPTER THIRTY-ONE

Another word for perfection is paralysis.

Winston Churchill

Many years ago, a friend who was having a substance abuse problem asked me if I would go with him to an AA meeting. I knew enough about the program to expect to see troubled people spill their guts in front of other troubled people, and I felt some anxiety about seeing myself as a part of it. Going in, I unconsciously armored myself with a mantra: "I am not like these people, I am not like these people, I am not like these people," relieved that I would not be called upon to speak – an elevated bystander. But when I listened to them bare their souls, I was not so elevated and fought to keep tears out of my eyes. They weren't just talking about themselves, they were talking about *me*.

The most memorable time came when a thirty-something woman spoke about the shattering end to a recent abusive relationship. She had obviously once been a pretty woman, but with her pockmarked face, bleached hair, and rumpled dress, she had the look of someone raised behind a country bar. As she finished her story and hung her head, a man across the room asked, "Can you call on your higher power?" She raised her head, looked him in the eye and responded in a firm voice, "Yeah, but God's up there and I'm down here."

I understood. In church, I was asked to relate to God and His son Jesus, who were so perfect they needed to be worshiped. In Zen, I was to be inspired by the possibility of achieving satori, whereupon I would, in a flash of white light, bypass all the messy internal struggle that plagued my life. In both cases, it was a bridge too far.

No one knows what Jesus was really like. All we have are four contradictory texts, written many years after His death, but it would be surprising if His disciples didn't clean Him up for presentation to the outside world. To the extent they sanitized Jesus, they insulated me from what He had to tell me. In fact, the first time I had any inkling that Christianity had anything to say to me came not in church but when I saw the play *Jesus Christ Superstar*. The pivotal scene for me was when Jesus is up on the mountain singing to God, bemoaning how, at the beginning, He didn't know what He was getting into, and He sings, "When we started..." and then He corrects himself, and sings accusingly, "*We* didn't start, *You* started..." Jesus is confused, discouraged, and resentful of His fate – in other words, He's human. From that moment on, I could at least begin to identify with Jesus and therefore *like* Him.

As for satori, I do not doubt that it would be an amazing thing to experience, but my brush with Zen practice and monasteries left me feeling that it was too good, at least for me. How can something be too good? If it becomes another one of my brain's primitives. Like Jesus, the Zen master represented a template of unattainable perfection that seemed to leave us students on the outside with our noses pressed up against the glass.

In a church or monastery, it's easy enough for me to become an elevated bystander, standing back from my everyday existence, thinking how much better I could be in the outside world. But once I exit the door, I find the messy world out there hasn't changed while I was gone *and neither has my ability to deal with it*. My brain has taken those inspiring ideas and converted them into something so "up there" that they can't survive down here.

I know when I feel good about my behavior, and I know what kind of behavior I am drawn to in others, and neither is anything like perfection or even previously defined. That behavior is not described on a stone tablet, rather it is more in the way of a rolling acknowledgement of how silly we all are so much of the time. It's amazing how that realization takes the pressure off. Suddenly we're all just in this together – open, loving, laughing.

I have come to think of the notion of perfection not as a goal, but as an obstacle. For most of my life, my brain has been handicapping me, other people and nature itself, and none of them measure up.

CHAPTER THIRTY-TWO

The devil made me do it.

Flip Wilson

I love early religious music – plainchants, renaissance choral music – sung in languages I do not understand that can take me to a place of pure inspiration and beauty for which I have no literal associations. At those times, I can briefly bypass my brain, have no need to think or do anything, and am, in the words of the hymn, "nearer my God to thee." In that place I may have some small inkling of what the iconic religious sages – Buddha, Jesus, Mohammed – must have experienced. But it's hard to stay in that place. My brain just can't get its arms around *God*, and wants to get on with calculating how to protect myself and improve my future.

That same pattern can be seen by looking at the history of the established religions that bear those sage's names. I suspect that those sages had an extraordinary ability to stay in that "God place," which allowed them to provide the original inspiration that spawned great movements. But, like all humans, they had finite lifespans, and that original inspiration had to be handed off to followers, most of whom, like me, had trouble staying in that place. Yet, even when those followers weren't in that place, many of them continued to build dogma, rules and institutions – and in the process, their own temporal power – all the while claiming the authority of God in doing so.

All too often, this has led to a slippery slope, going from wanting to be like God, to wanting God to be like them, and then to putting Him in harness. Once God is in that harness, it is a small step to seeing that you have a blank check regarding the bounds of humanity, because you're only following His instructions.

This, from Deuteronomy 20:10 of the Christian Old Testament:

"… as for the towns of these peoples that the Lord your God is giving you as an inheritance, you must not let anything that breathes remain alive. You shall annihilate them…just as the Lord your God has commanded, so that they may not teach you to do all the abhorrent things that they do for their gods…"

And, more recently, from the final written instructions given to the September 11 hijackers:

"When you enter the plane:

God, I trust in you. God, I lay myself in your hands. I ask with the light of your faith that has lit the whole world and lightened the darkness on this earth, to guide me until you approve of me. And once you do, that's my ultimate goal."

I can relate to those terrorists. At many times in my life, their behavior has been my behavior, writ small. An example is how I've treated my wives when I felt threatened. With Barbara, I knew she felt trapped and overwhelmed as a mother and needed some help with parenting so she could get out of the house and get some other kind of fulfillment. But until she fell apart emotionally, when it was too late, I intimidated her into playing the role that accommodated my needs and fears. The children were, like the tenants of the World Trade Center towers, collateral damage. As for Pat, she's not given to falling apart, but she can be hurt. Sometimes, when we've had arguments, I didn't just try to win the debate, but went for the jugular, making accusations about her behavior in the past having nothing to do with the present issue, just to inflict pain – a kind of mini terrorist attack.

On these occasions, I didn't claim to be acting on God's orders, but did much the same, looking down from the high horse of moral superiority. Of course, there was nothing moral in it. The instructions I was following were issued by a brain designed to enable ruthless animal competition.

It makes me understand the Christian doctrines of "born in sin." We're all sinners in our thoughts, and that bleeds out into our external behavior across the whole range of human experience.

So, what about *God*'s instructions? I believe the answer is that He doesn't issue instructions. Instead, He asks a question: "Who are you right now?"

CHAPTER THIRTY-THREE

It's not enough to succeed, others must fail.

Gore Vidal

If religion wasn't something I could bring into my life when I was young, at least my dad's idea that my goal should be to get things that other people didn't have offered a clearly defined path. It dovetailed neatly with his opinion that other people were not to be trusted – in effect: "I know those bastards are no good because they're trying to do to me what I'm trying to do to them."

It also dovetails with how our calculator brains see the world. When you first learn arithmetic in school, you are told that if you have four and take away two, there will only be two left. In any finite universe, a subtraction means there's less remaining. Either you get it or I get it, but not both. If two primitive humans wanted the only cave around, only one would get it – that's the math and that's the psychology. With that kind of outlook it's difficult to wish the best for your fellow human beings. This zero-sum computational mentality dogged me for much of my life, leaving me feeling impotent and afraid.

Fortunately, I inherited only part of Dad's attitude. I didn't want to beat other people – I actually liked them and wanted them to be happy. I just didn't want to *lose*. Unfortunately, that was bad enough. The fear of failure haunted me. It was those voices in my head – like this imagined conversation between two of my former acquaintances from college:

"Hey, remember that guy Shep McKenney, who was on the debate team at William and Mary?"

"Sure. How he wound up owning the Hinckley Company I never could understand."

"Turns out he couldn't understand it either. I heard he had to lay off most of the employees and is filing for bankruptcy."

"If he's broke, that hot wife of his isn't going to stick around for long."

Those terrible voices in my brain made me want to just retreat and disengage from any sort of competition or comparison. Yet I had to face the world around me, and in that world, competition is everywhere, from the schoolyard to the College of Cardinals. And when it comes to the ability to compete, we are not all one. Not only do differences in physical makeup divide us, but we also don't come equipped with equal brains. Even though we seem to be the winners of the evolutionary contest, nature is still throwing up random genetic variations that are the very foundation of that contest. There are so many people out there naturally superior to me – better-looking and smarter. My adding-machine brain kept telling me that there's only so much to get out there, and the superior people were going to get it.

But if I'm not afraid of losing, can I still drive myself to do the hard things it takes to compete? Is fear a necessary ingredient of success? There is no doubt that visceral fear, as in ducking when someone tries to hit you in the head, is a useful instinct. But what about fear as a necessary emotion for achievement? Certainly, that was the message I received as a child when I was warned not to "fall short."

Yet, I have long known that fear dumbs me down, inhibiting my ability to inspire myself and those around me. Could I approach competition in an entirely different way? Is it possible to succeed as a Chief Asker of Dumb Questions?

CHAPTER THIRTY-FOUR

As I would not be a slave So I would not be a master.

Abraham Lincoln

When we started our gyro company, we thought we could produce a product in two years and a profit in four. Those numbers turned out to be five and ten. What happened? First, we grossly underestimated the technical challenges in creating such a device, which in some ways is as difficult to engineer and manufacture as a jet engine. Second, we didn't just have to build a gyro, we had to build an organization, including engineering, supply chain, volume manufacturing, distribution, sales, product support, and finance, all with an international reach. Third, we had no idea how long it would take to get the boating public to accept something so unintuitive and unfamiliar.

In early 2007 we changed the company name to Seakeeper, thinking that "Gearloose" might not be a comforting name for a heavy flywheel spinning at ten thousand rpm. Armed with serial number one of the Seakeeper Gyro, I went to one of the largest fishing tournaments on the East Coast to introduce it, complete with information booth and demonstrator boat. In three days, I had one person come to our booth, and they were looking for someone else's booth. When we started to exhibit at major boat shows, the overwhelming (or, I should say underwhelming) reaction was for people to walk by our display, glance at the gyro, and shake their heads as they kept on going. Maybe all those people thought it was a gimmick. Yet when we could convince someone to go out on our demonstrator boat and experience what the gyro could do, a frequent comment was, "Oh, my God!"

Finally, we got a large order from one of the biggest boatbuilders in the world, and we thought we were on our way. Then the 2008 worldwide economic meltdown happened and the order was cancelled. By 2011, nine years into our enterprise, we still hadn't made a profit, I had put millions of dollars into the company and was forced to mortgage the farm. For the third time in my professional life, I was facing bankruptcy. Only a last-minute merciful infusion of cash from one of our outside investors saved us (and me).

Then, slowly, painfully slowly, we began to get orders, barely alive, until in 2013 we made a small profit. After that, the boating community increasingly began to get what we had believed in all along. As of this writing (2022), many thousands of Seakeeper gyros are installed on boats worldwide and the Seakeeper company is valued at more than a billion dollars.

As with my other two entrepreneurial ventures, I had gone through a near-death experience. And, like the other two times, through it all my brain kept screaming that the world was ending. The difference this time was that I knew the screamer wasn't *me*, which gave me a set of virtual earmuffs that permitted me to exude a confidence and level of trust in other people that wouldn't have been possible otherwise. That trust wasn't just my handing out assignments and then walking away, but something more fundamental. I was willing to be vulnerable, to acknowledge how much I didn't know. I didn't want to be the master, and I didn't want them to be slaves. That didn't mean I wasn't exercising power, just not the dictatorial kind. My dumb questions let my coworkers know they didn't just need me, but that I needed them and the value of the answers to those dumb questions that only they could provide. *Let's help this guy.*

I made myself lovable, so they loved me, and I, in turn, loved them. They were happy with me and I was happy with them. That happiness created a safe space in which all of us could bring out the best in ourselves, allowing a team of company leaders to come into being that is beyond anything I have ever seen in terms of competence and productivity and who create great products and services that consumers want to buy. I've learned that shared happiness doesn't just feel good in the present, it's productive, creating positive external results in the future.

The Seakeeper experience has left me with a new understanding of one particular word: "expert." In the course of working through the difficult technical problems with the gyro, we employed many consultants in fields such as high-speed bearings, vacuums and computerized controls. In all of those cases, those "experts" supplied some baseline information that was helpful but, to a surprising degree, they were unable to provide solutions to the problems. Instead, we, the "beginners" in these "specialized" fields, through trial and error, sorted out what needed to be done. The experts couldn't hand us the combination to the safe; instead, we had to sand our fingertips and divine it ourselves. The experts have their databases and algorithms, but we got close, not only to the gyro, but also to our coworkers in an intimate way.

It makes me think about my experience raising children. At the time, I struggled to find answers, reading books written by "experts" who could tell me how to do it. What I didn't do was to get close enough to those children to allow human exploration – owning what I didn't know, creating a safe space, and, in the process, unlocking their latent creative power and mine.

I believe that the way to get things done is the same way to conduct a human life – not being a master, but seeing myself as a part of a fluid, unending puzzle, knowing that humility, not superiority, is the way to have things come right.

It is also creation. Before we started Seakeeper, virtually no one had heard of control moment gyroscopes. When we built them, people saw something that had come out of nowhere, and they wanted it. The bauxite (aluminum ore), iron ore and silicon that make up the parts could just have easily stayed in the ground and no one would have known the difference. The difference had nothing to do with finite, zero-sum resources, but came from human beings opening up to excitement. That difference has resulted in several thousand people being employed directly and indirectly by Seakeeper, people who get up in the morning with something useful to do – supporting their families, paying taxes that supports government and spending money that supports all kinds of businesses – which, in turn, employ people who participate in the same cycle. Beyond that, the gyro has created a new and better experience for boaters, which will encourage more people to want boats, resulting in more boats, marinas and boating accessories, and propagating that cycle in all directions, like ripples from a pebble dropped in still water.

CHAPTER THIRTY-FIVE

If there were no God
It would be necessary to invent Him.

Voltaire

When I began commuting from Maryland to Maine by piloting my own plane, I was introduced to a different kind of flying, one in which I was an amateur in a professional's world. Not only was I operating at altitudes normally reserved for large commercial aircraft (around five miles up), but I was transiting some of the most congested airspace in the world, the Northeast Corridor of the United States. At those altitudes, strict air traffic control is a necessity and the law requires that all flight plans be filed and approved. Moreover, weather and other variables often necessitate changes in flight plans in this complex, always fluid, puzzle, and in order to have the requisite separation between planes these variations must come from a central, coordinated source – the federal air traffic controllers.

These people not only have grave responsibility, they also possess dictatorial power. Seated in upholstered chairs in darkened rooms, staring at glowing radar screens, they are the sole repository of information regarding the big picture – only they know where all those other planes are out there and what they are doing, so only they can call the plays.

For the pilot in the sky, these remote, unseen people are known only by their clipped, cryptic instructions: "American 28 Heavy cleared to flight level 240, come to heading 030 until intercept with airway 12, contact Philadelphia center on 123.5" – all said with a rapidity that makes the words comprehensible only to the initiated. For the pilot, these instructions are not for him to reason why, but only to do or die – not merely in the sense that disobeying could lead to an accident, but also because failure to conform can lead to later disciplinary action, including loss of his license to fly, which for a career pilot is something like death.

No one, including the pilots, contends that the imposition of central authority can be avoided, but there can be moments when those same pilots suspect that controllers exercise their godlike powers in an unnecessarily arbitrary way in order to simplify their own jobs and thus lighten their workload. For the subservient airline pilot, bouncing around in the turbulence with a bunch of anxious passengers in the back, worried about how much fuel he has left, concerned about making his son's Little League game, being routed around his elbow to get to his thumb can be a maddening experience.

Since I was flying at altitudes where these communications were taking place, I was on the same radio frequencies and got to hear the often imperious tone of the controllers and the not-so-subtle inflection of frustration and impotence in the voices of the pilots. Once, when I was coming home from Maine during a particularly bad period of weather and thus disrupted flight plans, I was eavesdropping on a continuing dialogue between a Delta pilot and the New York controller, in which the pilot kept asking when he would be allowed to exit the holding pattern (in effect, flying in circles) which he had been ordered to be in for some time. Finally, after several inquiries which met with no satisfactory response from the controller, the pilot came back on the frequency and said he had a different question.

The impatient controller barked, "Go ahead."

The pilot asked, "Am I up here because you're down there, or are you down there because I'm up here?"

That's a good question to ask about God. Who is serving whom, and what's the ultimate point of the exercise?

It is reasonable to think that primitive humans were somewhat in the position of the airline pilot in that they were dealing with a difficult and dangerous environment full of unknowns and even inexplicable senselessness, one which they felt compelled to assume was set in motion by an unseen intelligence that had access to information and power that they did not, and whose instructions they could disobey only at their peril. This whole thing – human existence – is pretty spooky, and somebody up there must know what's going on, and maybe He'll even take care of us if only we can figure out what He wants us to do.

But what if there isn't?

Let me suggest another way to think about it. Humans of thousands of years ago had computers in their heads too – in fact, ones just as large and powerful as ours – and those computers wanted to solve the problem of an uncertain, dangerous world.

What if those ancient humans set their brains to work on solving this problem of how to relate to the world as they knew it, and it came up with a *computer interface* that seemed to answer those otherwise unanswerable questions. That interface could reduce reality to something their computers could comprehend – finite beginnings and ends and make reality computer-friendly by supplying reasons and solutions. God put me in this infernal holding pattern for good reasons known only to Him, and if I will be subservient and obedient and follow His instructions, I will have a safe landing after all. In other words, God didn't engineer us down here, but rather our brains engineered Him up there to solve a problem we have down here – the intolerably unpredictable nature of life itself.

CHAPTER THIRTY-SIX

Life isn't doing a sum, it's painting a picture.

Oliver Wendell Holmes Jr.

The idea of brain as computer is not new, but it is controversial, at least in the field of psychology, where it is sometimes called the "despised computer metaphor." Part of it seems to be based on the fear that it conjures up a vision of human brains as indelibly programmed computers, which in turn renders their owners not responsible for their behavior – the Darwinian defense for rape. *I* didn't do it – my computer brain, programmed by evolution to encourage the strongest to reproduce, did it.

And part of it is a distinction without a difference. No, brains are not digital in the way a laptop is, but almost entirely analog; no, brains are much more capable of parallel processing (doing many things at once) than a laptop is; no, a brain is almost entirely chemical and the laptop is purely electrical; no, a laptop is fast and brains are slow; and, no, brains don't come in a cardboard box.

What, after all, is a computer? It is a device that uses a database and algorithms to solve problems. *That's what the brain is.* A computer is not a *metaphor* for the brain, rather, the brain is literally a computer, or at least a system of them. Humans didn't invent computers, nature did – no mechanism is more ubiquitous in the animal world and no bird could fly or fish swim without them. Like the God of the Old Testament, the computers in our heads created the computers on our desks *in their own image*. To take the air traffic controller analogy a step further, is there a brain in my head because there is a computer on my desk, or vice versa?

When, around the middle of the twentieth century, manmade computers came into general use, science fiction writers were quick to jump on the possibility of these devices mutating into an evil intelligence that oppresses or even destroys humanity. Stanley Kubrick's movie *2001: A Space Odyssey*, the most famous of this genre, has Hal, the spaceship's onboard mega-computer, develop human feelings and jealousies to the point where it murders crewmembers. And it wasn't just science fiction writers – around that time there began genuine speculation in many quarters that computers might become so powerful they could someday take over and become tyrants over humankind.

In a sense, that talk was tacit recognition that computers are like us. After all, people weren't talking about cars or washing machines taking over. Instead, they recognized that computers, are, at the very least, brain extenders that compound our ability to calculate, and if they can think the way we think, maybe they can act as we act. And history and everyday experience shows that, in human society, tyranny is an ever-present threat.

Yet in the twenty-first century, even as computers have become enormously more powerful and pervasive, there is less of that talk. The reason, I believe, is that as we become more familiar with them, we are coming to understand that electronic computers don't intend *anything*, but are dependent on us for instructions.

One illustration of this is how often manmade computers need to be *updated*. This is not only adapting to new circumstances or adding new features, but more often than not, simply tweaking them to conform to our intentions. As a person who has been professionally involved in complex software development for the last fifteen years, I can testify that the process of refinement is never-ending. The software in my electric car was developed by hundreds of software engineers over many years of refinement, yet I am constantly getting updates over the internet, most of which are "fixes."

Part of the problem is that when layering thousands of algorithms on top of each other it's hard to know how they'll interact. Another is that the computer is always looking for certainty, something that can be hard to come by in everyday experience. In the end, manmade computers are dependent on us to continually provide fixes that make them conform to the functions that we originally intended.

In the case of our brains, we didn't *intend* their function in the first place, which was to enable the continuity of animal existence in a primitive environment. What we intend in the modern world is to live a decent, fulfilling human life. When it comes to understanding the ultimate value of our existence, we've been handed an abacus when we need a paintbrush.

CHAPTER THIRTY- SEVEN

Physician, heal thyself.

Jesus Christ

In the spring of 1970, while walking alone along the shore of the waterfront property Barbara and I had recently bought, I looked back at our handsome, just-finished house and two gleaming new cars parked in the driveway, and I reflected on the fact that I had just received an unsolicited increase in my partnership share at the law firm.

Then the thought came to me unbidden: *Only bad things can happen now because all the good things have already happened.* The pitiful fact was that I saw myself as someone who had overachieved to the point of being way out on a limb, precariously lucky, with no place to go but down. Fetching up on this realization hit me with a dull thud, and while I didn't know what to do about it I had to come to grips with the fact that I was emotionally sick. The career change and divorce that shortly followed weren't a prescription for curing that disease, rather a kind of thrashing around in the dark, knowing something had to change.

"Disease" is one of those words that defines itself – you are not at ease because you are suffering. In common usage it describes a condition that only affects certain people at certain times and visibly stands out in a way that makes it amenable to identification and treatment. In other words, it's not normal.

My disease, however, was normal, and the flare-up of ennui I just described merely a particularly absurd symptom of it. I was suffering from something I've seen around me all my life: humans allowing their brains to so limit and define what is good and bad in the present, and possible in the future, that they suffer, first from impotence, and then from depressing angst. This disease, I believe, is far more damaging to our species than any abnormal physical condition, but we accept it because it is so universal that it seems to be the "human condition."

Can we choose *not* to be in that condition? Can we choose, from moment to moment, what our brains are doing? Certainly we can when it comes to "executive" function. If I choose to end my writing session right now, my brain has my body carrying out my choice exactly the way I want, moving the mouse on the pad, clicking the "x" in the upper right hand of the computer screen, clicking "save," then moving on to wash out my coffee cup, put on my coat, and go out the door, my choice being carried out automatically.

But when it comes to my sense of wellbeing, it's different. Things happen automatically here too, but not necessarily in response to a choice I've made. When it comes to addressing the value of my life, all too often, *my brain chooses* in its mindless way, adding, dividing and subtracting with a blizzard of information and algorithms that I can't see through, my emotions like a leaf in the wind, rising and falling, twisting and turning.

Is there any escape from this diseased condition? There is, but it requires choosing, in the moment, who's in charge. Is it me, or is it my brain?

There is a medical parallel here. It is an expression much used in the military regarding the urgency of treating traumatic injury, which has also been applied to strokes and heart attacks. The term is "the golden hour," after which it's too late. In the case of mental disease, the golden time is not an hour, or a minute, but more like a few seconds. So ingrained, habituated and programmed is my brain to running my life that it is very difficult to rein it in once it takes over. So, the cure any time I'm feeling diseased is to stop, regardless of what is happening around me, and ask myself, *Is this what I want to feel?*

So I believe there is an escape, but it requires the ability to visualize where those mindless choices are coming from, which is not from *I*, but from *it*. I can't make a choice if I don't know I have one. It then calls for asking the question, What's good about those fearful, negative emotions? To elaborate, what's good about anxiety, anger, disappointment or feelings of inferiority (or its mirror image, arrogance)? What constructive purpose do they serve for me or, for that matter, anyone around me? And I know this: when I experience those emotions, I model their effects, making my disease communicable.

Would I choose to have those feelings if I knew I had a choice? It may *feel* like those emotions are thrust on me by external circumstances, but if they're not, why not make a good choice?

Even in the case of grief, will I choose to suffer from a sense of loss (which is no help to anyone, including the deceased), or feel gratitude that I had the relationship at all? That, in the end (the very end), is what good eulogies are all about.

The realization that this disease of helplessness is susceptible to being cured takes the concept of free will to the most profound level, far beyond finite choices such as what will I wear today, or what career will I choose; rather, it is becoming the creator of my own life. In this way of thinking, the "human condition" is not one of impotence, but of power.

CHAPTER THIRTY - EIGHT

We need education in the obvious more than investigation
of the obscure.

Oliver Wendell Holmes, Jr.

Actually, there was an attempt back there to help me avoid dis-ease, but only of the physical kind. It was called Health Class, and in it we learned about the organs of our bodies – what they were there for and how they functioned. We also received instruction on how to manage those organs – brush our teeth, eat the right foods, exercise, et cetera - but as I recall, there was one organ that received only scant attention, and it is the one that manages all the others.

That's not surprising in the sense that those other organs were easier to understand because we had analogs for them – the heart is a pump, the lungs are bellows, the kidneys are filters, and our skeleton is the structure of our bodies like the structure of a building – giving a reasonably clear notion of how they worked. In the absence of that analog, our brains were what engineers call a "black box" – you can see the results of what it's doing, but how it's doing it is a mystery.

But today, we do have a brain analog in the form of personal computers, and because we are, from an early age, so caught up the use of those computers, that analog is not just intellectual but also experiential. Not only are their functional mechanics very similar to our brains but, like our brains, they are tools that we use to inform and navigate our lives.

That analog is crucial because it relates our brains to a *thing* with a defined role, the essential mechanics of which are well understood. This allows the realization that our brains are not the mystery, but the mystery is what our brains don't get. And since love, enthusiasm, creativity and all that other good stuff that can't be defined or predicted will always be mysterious, that covers a lot of ground.

But can you teach mystery? Buddha didn't think so. When he finally went *in there* and experienced his own transcendence, his first thought was, *This cannot be taught.* How do you teach something that can't be seen, defined or explained in the way we teach geography and math? How do you take apart and analyze something that is utterly seamless? I don't think you can.

What we can do is to acknowledge that *God* is in every one of us in a way that can never be described or measured, with no apologies for all the perversions that have been done in the name of God and religion. And, having made that acknowledgement, there is something that can be taught, which is what separates us from that *God* that is patiently waiting inside us. This is teaching the brain to stay within its proper role – which the brain can be taught, just as we teach it to perform management in other aspects of our lives. If I can teach it to tie my shoelaces, I can teach it to stop messing up my life.

CHAPTER THIRTY - NINE

When I was five years old my mother always told me that
happiness was the key to life. When I went to school, they
asked me what I wanted to be when I grew up. I wrote down
"happy." They told me I didn't understand the assignment,
and I told them they didn't understand life.

John Lennon

A nd what about our children?

We want to educate them, give them the tools to be able to have a
successful life. And, to the extent we can measure the acquisition of those
tools, we're doing an increasingly good job of that. Like many of my
contemporaries, I have speculated that the "me" of sixty years ago would
have little chance of getting into my alma mater of today, much less
succeed there. The amount of information and analysis that students of
today have to learn and recall on tests is, by any historical standard, truly
astonishing. It is also astonishing how much pressure it puts on students
who have varying genetic capabilities and cultural backgrounds, trying to
measure them by a one-size-fits-all yardstick.

So, given all that, are we doing an increasingly good job of preparing them
for a successful life? Insofar as happiness is the "test" of a successful life,
there is considerable evidence that we are not. To illustrate, the number

of college students requesting therapy and counseling has doubled in just the last four or five years. A friend of mine who leads one of the most prestigious public universities in the country tells me that fully a third of the incoming students are taking some kind of (prescription) mind-altering drug. Suicide is the second-leading cause of death for persons aged ten to thirty-four. There is an accelerating increase in diagnosable mental health problems and a corresponding decrease in the ability of many young people to manage the everyday bumps in the road of life.

We're going faster and faster in supplying information to those students, but leaving them lost in that we don't seem to be able to help them feel secure and comfortable in their own skin, particularly in an environment in which competitive ranking and testing can take on a life-or-death character.

What is required is to address the underlying issue of what a good life is – something not measurable or quantifiable by grades in school or accomplishments afterward, but having an inner strength that accepts and appreciates the inevitable differences in us and the unavoidable uncertainties in the external world. We need a new kind of "Health Class."

And how would the thrust of this health class be different from what is offered in our present educational system? Allow me to suggest these possibilities:

It would teach them about the most important organ of their bodies, how it came to be, what it was designed to do, and how to use it and enjoy it, but always see it as a tool that must serve and not rule.

It would put speculative goals for the future in perspective, emphasizing what goal is at all, which is ongoing present happiness. Yet the emphasis on present experience would not diminish the opportunity for future achievement, but rather increase the likelihood of it – letting them know that it's like making a car trip at night: you can only see as far as your headlights, but by doing that you are able to make it the whole way.

It would be built around the realization that we're all equal in having an ultimate self that knows what is good and right, independent of the body or brain we were born with, recognizing that the most important aspect of intelligence is the ability, in the moment, to separate the important from the unimportant.

There would be individualized lab work, asking the student to look into their own interior experience so as to create a personal owner's manual for their brains that works for their own particular psychological situation.

It would put the rest of the educational system in perspective, allowing the student to see that it is not their master, but a servant of their individual capabilities and interests, and not allow it to act as measure of their personal worth.

Rather than emphasize the acquisition of clearly defined information and explanations, it would invite the student to make friends with mystery.

I believe the best thing we can do for our children is to let them know that their main task in this life is to be happy, and how to navigate around the obstacles to that happiness.

CHAPTER FORTY

In so far as we are animals, our business is at all costs to
survive. To make biological survival possible, mind at large
has to be funneled through the reducing valve of the brain
and nervous system. What comes out at the other end is a
measly trickle of the kind of consciousness which will help us
stay alive on the surface of this particular planet.

Aldous Huxley

In this chapter I will present some additional thoughts on how seeing
our brains for what they are can change how we see ourselves and the
world around us.

We need an alternative Book of Genesis that explains how all life on
Earth, including us, was created by a competition to separate winners
from losers. That creation story provides a basis for understanding the
purpose for which our brains were created, and, thus, what we've got to
work with. This can then be contrasted with our purpose, which is to get
beyond that desperate competition and experience joy, love, excitement
– in other words, happiness.

We also need an alternative picture of heaven. The better life that is
waiting for us is just that, not perfect, not reduced to a computational
primitive, and the world is never going to arrange itself around our

specific desires. The lion is going to continue to eat the lamb, and one of our jobs in this life is to appreciate this beautiful world that evolution, for all of its ruthlessness, has given us, loving the lion as much as the lamb. Heaven is not an escape from an unsatisfactory present, but being in accord with the world just as it is. It is not that we don't work to make the exterior world better, but that heaven is not to be found in that future result, but in who we are while we're doing that work.

In many ways, we need to anticipate the future just as much as primitive human beings did. Almost every move we make, be it paying utility bills, obeying traffic signals or going to work in the morning, is a calculated act, designed to lead to a desirable future result. These are functions that are indispensable to our continued physical existence for which we are utterly dependent on the tool in our heads. Yet all this does is engineer the canvas. It is up to us to be the artist who paints on it.

Evolution in the past was a contest in which only a tiny percentage of the contestants (genetically speaking) made it through, and the winners' behavioral triggers had to be hardwired to their bodies through their nervous system to elicit the most intense and immediate responses – the quick and the dead. As with championship athletes, everything was geared to achieve one crucial, finite result. So, when we go to overrule those intense responses and just open up to what life has to offer, our brains fight back, not just insisting and yelling at us, but often sabotaging our bodies, leaving us physically diseased. Those behavioral triggers also sabotage our relations with other human beings, insisting on putting on threat displays, just as lower animals do, to set limits to protect ourselves. Yet, being cold, judgmental or angry is not just destructive, it's unnecessary. When setting limits, a door is just as closed if it is closed gently as when it is slammed.

Computers want certainty. We can use computers –the ones in our heads and the ones we make – to harness limited mechanical certainty to provide a foundation for our existence, but the trajectory of our lives is anything but certain. So, if uncertainty is not going to come to us, we can go to it, and embrace it, recognizing that the best things in life are surprises, even if they don't look like it at first.

A way to think about why our brains don't care about us is to consider that the evolutionary process that designed our brains didn't care about individuals, but about *statistics* – what particular genetic characteristic would, over many individuals, emerge as the most able to promote survival and reproduction in a wide variety of situations. It was a process of refinement built on sacrificing large number of individuals to select a few, who would then move on to the next stage of sacrifice and refinement. As indispensable to our bare existence as they are, they are not our friends, nor were they designed to be. In computer-speak, they are not "user- friendly."

The traditional philosophical and religious separation between the secular and the spiritual is one of the brain's ways of dealing with mystery. As an intellectual distinction, it is so arm's length, it doesn't have much impact on our happiness. But it is the tip of an iceberg that does, which is the persistent idea that the portal to a better life is to be found somewhere beyond our ordinary, workaday world, whether it's a church, a monastery, a pilgrimage to a holy place, listening to an inspiring speech or reading a self-help book. Yet, as uplifting as these extraordinary experiences may be, they are perishable. On Sunday we are inspired by a glimpse of just how good life can be, and then go to work on Monday, when that inspiration perishes in the flames of the doubts and worries triggered by everyday events and associations. But Monday is when our lives are lived out, and if we want more than a glimpse of that better life, we need to understand how our lives ebb away, not from body blows, but from being pecked to death: *I hope the traffic's not bad tonight; Global warming is going to destroy the planet; Why did she say that?; This pain in my shoulder could be cancer; I need to give up trying because this can't turn out well.* We don't have to go looking for that portal somewhere else – it's always been inside us – we just need to constantly unclog it.

We should think of our brains the way we think about inanimate tools we use in everyday life. So, for example, we can compare them to a washing machine, which comes with an owner's manual, the very first pages of which warn you that *this thing can hurt you if not used properly.* In the case of the washing machine, that could be electrocution, flooding the floor, or simply ruining your clothes. In the case of our brains, the hurt is illustrated by the dis-ease that can be seen all around us. We want the washing machine to do what we want it to do without causing a bunch of problems. *Just wash the damn clothes.* Modern washing machines are reasonably trouble-free – modern brains, not at all.

Whatever culture we come from, whatever color we are, whatever our sex, whatever genetic makeup we've been handed, we're all alike in this way: we all have brains, we all have electronic computers, and we all have an inner self that knows what is good and right. That means we can share a way of thinking about how to make our lives better that is independent of any traditional boundaries or unnecessary judgments, providing a commonality that strips away the quantitative aspects of our differences.

CHAPTER FORTY- ONE

If the doors of perception were cleansed, everything would
appear to man as it is, infinite.

William Blake

We humans are in a situation we've never been in before. We are the Olympic champions of the evolutionary contest and dominate the planet. Our outward circumstances, at least in the industrialized world, are not just a quantum leap beyond what our primitive ancestors experienced, but also far better than could have been imagined until very recently. Today, people below the poverty line live longer, safer, healthier lives than royalty of two hundred years ago. You'd think we'd all be walking around with smiles on our faces, expressing gratitude for how great things are.

But we're not.

Despite the ever-accelerating technological developments that are continuing to transform the exterior experience of human life, the inner experience – the one that matters –isn't changing much. All of our brilliance in rearranging our physical environment is not advancing the cause of getting our lives and the world around us to conform to our hopes and expectations. Virtually every survey that attempts to measure such things indicates that people in the United States are, if anything, becoming more pessimistic and distrustful of other people.

Even our most focused efforts to meet the needs of the inner human don't seem to be improving things. Despite the proliferation of school psychologists, counseling services, anti-depressant drugs, and the utter explosion of self-help books, angst is, if anything, on the rise. The Centers for Disease Control reports that, over the last twenty years, suicide rates in the United States, across most ethnic and age groups, are up twenty-five percent.

Of course, there is joy out there – but it remains as ephemeral as the full belly of *Homo erectus*. An insidious dynamic is that no matter how many problems are solved, new ones magically appear – something that has been called the Progress Paradox. If you look at the front page of a newspaper of today compared to one of a hundred years ago, the world of today doesn't look any happier or less threatening. In fact, you don't even have to look at newspapers. With the advent of the internet-augmented twenty-four-hour news cycle, there is an inexhaustible, inescapable supply of bad news.

But why is most of that news bad? One answer is the traditional saying in journalism that, "If it bleeds, it leads." Yet that only addresses the reality that the media is giving us what we want. But do we want "bad"? Of course *we* don't. Yes, bad news sells, but for the first time in human history we have a way of understanding who the buyer is – a machine designed to navigate around existential threats and hence on the constant lookout for them.

We have escaped the desperate circumstances of our ancestors, but so far, we haven't been able to escape desperation itself. In a sense, we're fighting the same battles they fought, except the battlefield has changed: they battled exterior threats and we're battling interior threats.

Attempts to deal with this interior struggle have, in fact, been going on since the rise of civilization in the form of religion, going back at least to the Bronze Age in the Indus Valley in present-day India. What, after all, is religion but an attempt to find some significance in life beyond the struggle for animal survival – setting out to find some purpose, whether it's following the instructions of an all-knowing god or simply finding out what's good about living at all in an environment that seems so troublesome? Across the board, the best idea religion has given us is that we have an unseen self that can connect with and experience ultimate value. In the words of Joseph Campbell, "All religions are true in this sense – they all reach for transcendence." And if we don't have religion, or some other way of thinking about our existence that allows us to experience value in being alive, we might as well be vegetables.

But religion, for all the good it has done, has had a hard time from the beginning, tending to devolve into hierarchy and tribalism, looking right past the ultimate self that we all share. It has done that so often because however insightful the initial impulse, it had to be run through a calculating device designed to foster competition, pulling us apart instead of together.

That calculating device is a kind of glass ceiling that we unwittingly keep bumping into when we seek ultimate value, whether it's through organized religion or simply trying to do a better job of conducting our daily lives.

We've been playing the game without knowing the cards in our hands.

Now, for the first time in human history, we have the opportunity to understand what transcendence is: rising above the limitations of our brains. After thousands of years of searching, we have a totally new way to get to the root cause of why it is so hard to be happy.

CHAPTER FORTY-TWO

Most folks are about as happy as
they make up their minds to be.

Abraham Lincoln

As I entered my seventy-eighth year in the summer of 2019 I could look back on a remarkably healthy life, having had no significant illnesses or injuries and rarely even a cold. I had never spent the night in a hospital. But in September of that year my body was to let me know that couldn't last forever.

I was driving home from the grocery store when I felt a slight tightening in my neck and shoulders. Though not painful, it was enough to get my attention, so I called Dick Stephenson, my best doctor friend, to get my free medical consultation and he suggested going to the emergency room. That seemed like overkill given the mildness of the symptoms, but I didn't have a better idea so I went to the emergency room. When I got there, they did a CAT scan of my neck and shoulders, and while it didn't reveal anything in my neck and shoulders, there was something out of the ordinary at the upper part of my chest, and the doctor ordered a second scan covering that area.

What that second scan revealed was a ballooning of the aorta next to my heart (a "thoracic aortic aneurysm") that was subject to bursting at any time – a ticking fatal time bomb. Interestingly, they couldn't connect the symptoms that sent me to the hospital with the aneurysm and those symptoms never recurred. More interesting was the fact that I had no preconditions normally associated with aneurysms – high blood pressure, clogged arteries, tobacco use and family history. It was as if I had been struck by lightning – perfectly healthy one minute and mortally threatened the next.

An hour after the second scan I found myself strapped to a gurney in a coffin-like space in the back of a Medivac helicopter, headed to Washington Hospital Center, filled with a sense of wonder – could this be real, or was I dreaming? Pat managed to persuade the pilot to let her sit in the co-pilot's seat, and she reported that coming up on the darkened city lights at low altitude, she felt a remarkable sense of peace.

When we got to the hospital the atmosphere was quite friendly, almost as if we were being welcomed into someone's home. After they had gotten me into a bed we were interviewed by two nurses about my existing medications, and had a hilarious discussion of the merits of Viagra, the effects of which they seemed to have had considerable experience. A half-hour later the surgeon appeared and gave me a briefing that was a model of clarity – what my condition was, the surgery they intended to perform to fix it, the risks and aftereffects. I liked and trusted the man immediately.

The surgery that was performed on me two days later is one of the most dazzling examples of modern medical technology. In the simplest terms, they split my chest open, hooked me up to a heart-lung machine, temporarily disabling and replacing those two organs, repaired the damage, hooked me back up and sewed me up.

When I got back to my room after the surgery Pat was waiting for me and never left my side for the following three days of my hospital stay, during which she was unfailingly cheerful and drama-free. Getting me to the bathroom, helping me use it, and getting me back to bed with all those tubes and attachments, among other acquired skills, provided plenty of laughs. I think the staff at the hospital were glad to have us. *We all had a good time.*

Over the following six months I devoted myself to the most disciplined workout routine of my life – it turns out that lungs don't like being shut down, even briefly, and I had a lot of ground to make up. But at the end of that time I was in the best shape I had been in for years, an accomplishment from which I take considerable satisfaction.

My take on all this is that during that helicopter ride Pat and I decided to bring the best part of ourselves to the experience. Whatever the future held, we would not be victims of circumstance, but would act on the realization that what ultimately matters is not what happens out there but who we are in there. That meant that we would not let those brain voices rule us: *I can't believe this awful thing has happened; This has got be painful; What if I don't survive the surgery and, even if I do, I'll never be the same physically; I can't wait to get out of this hospital.* We didn't have to decide to be cheerful, and optimistic and funny; rather, that happened automatically when we ignored those destructive voices.

That heart surgery experience is a model for how I'm living my life now, walking around in a cocoon of self-awareness, much more focused on "in there" than "out there," constantly on the lookout for brain drama. I've come to think of my brain as an indispensable employee that refuses to stay within its job description, requiring constant supervision. The key word here is "employee" – it works for me, doing what I want it to do and nothing more. If this every-waking-moment practice sounds tedious, believe me it's not – rather, it's *liberating.* Before, I had no idea how much my freelancing brain was polluting my life.

And because I'm cleaning up the garbage in there, I'm also cleaning up my act out there – more considerate and open, always aware of the impact of my words on others.

It's not perfect. Many mornings I still wake up depressed, too groggy to wrestle my brain to the ground. Sometimes I blurt out negative things from long habit before I can catch myself. And there are times when I suffer from a vague background anxiety, like the muffled drum of a distant funeral march, too indistinct to identify and get my arms around.

But, for the most part, I'm the person I always wanted to be. That miracle is a result of having made it my life's work to constantly overrule my mindless brain, uncovering the still, small voice within me that always knows what's good and right. This book is my attempt to share that miracle with others in the hope that it will help them to be happier.

Made in the USA
Middletown, DE
25 September 2022

11182672R00106